BATTLE CRY

*A True Story of **Hope** and **Encouragement***

JORDYN GLASER

WESTBOW
PRESS®
A DIVISION OF THOMAS NELSON
& ZONDERVAN

WestBow Press books may be ordered through booksellers or by contacting:

WestBow Press
A Division of Thomas Nelson & Zondervan
1663 Liberty Drive
Bloomington, IN 47403
www.westbowpress.com
1 (866) 928-1240

ISBN: 978-1-9736-5332-5 (sc)
ISBN: 978-1-9736-5331-8 (hc)
ISBN: 978-1-9736-5333-2 (e)

Library of Congress Control Number: 2019901514

Print information available on the last page.

WestBow Press rev. date: 02/27/2019

Contents

Chapter 1   The Rescued 1

Chapter 2   Talking in the Quiet 12

Chapter 3   Taking Steps with Fear...................................25

Chapter 4   Building the Foundation 43

Chapter 5   Following the Detours 59

Chapter 6   Stepping Out of the Boat 81

Chapter 7   Surrendering 100

Chapter 8   The Call to Action....................................... 118

Battle Verses.. 139

Battle cry (noun): **a loud shout given by soldiers to frighten the enemy or to encourage their own side**

Dear reader,

I need to start off by saying I am *not* qualified to write this book. In fact, I tried to tell God no for a long time. I do not have a degree in writing. I do not have a long list of published works. I heavily rely on spell check and even that sometimes counts me as a hopeless cause. Frankly, I'm just not that special. But here's the thing—I *do* have a story to tell.

In fact, we all do.

Our lives are God's *battle cry*—our story is *His* victory!

Our life stories are battle cries meant to **encourage one another** and to **push back the enemy**—but they must be shared to do that.

I wrote these pages because I think it is time to rally. It is time to spread hope and remind fellow life soldiers of God's goodness even when the world feels heavy and the battle seems overwhelming. It is time to push back the enemy.

I hope these pages leave you with a renewed sense of strength and perseverance.

This is my personal battle cry.

This is my story.

Consider it pure joy, my brothers and sisters, whenever you face trials of many kinds, because you know that the testing of your faith produces perseverance. Let perseverance finish its work so that you may be mature and complete, not lacking anything.

—James 1:2–4 (NIV)

1 THE RESCUED

In the fall of 1983, Blaine and Julie became parents for the first time. The pregnancy was smooth, the delivery was quick, and they were soon home with their beautiful daughter. It was textbook. Or fairy tale.

They named their baby girl Rachel, and they glowed with pride at her perfection—like a small delicate doll. Julie dressed Rachel in multiple outfits a day. The proud mama then took pictures of each outfit to appreciate her work and bask in her happiness.

But the pictures were limited and would soon become cherished treasures because at ten days old, Rachel passed away.

An undetected heart defect cut her life short. Just like that, Blaine and Julie had lost their only daughter. When a wife loses her husband, she becomes a widow, when a husband loses his wife, he is a widower, and if a child loses her parents, she becomes an orphan.

There is just no word for parents who lose a child.

What do you do with an empty nursery and tiny, unworn clothes? How do you begin to rid a home of the smell of baby powder and Johnson & Johnson shampoo?

After Rachel died, family and friends gathered around Blaine and Julie through their grieving. They prayed for healing and ultimately prayed for a miracle. Less than two years later, their prayers were answered when a second baby girl was born.

That baby girl was me.

I was the child who followed the tragedy.

I was born in the spring of 1985. My parents lived one block from the hospital, yet I was still just minutes away from being delivered in their small blue car. Maybe we should have known in that moment that life wouldn't quite go according to plan.

After the loss of Rachel, the doctors were watching for similar problems. Rachel's heart defects were diagnosed as nongenetic defects, so the doctors believed there was not a high risk of it happening again. They performed a fetal echocardiogram during the pregnancy and conducted a full exam after birth. All looked clear.

Or so they believed.

When I was nine months old, my mother took me to an urgent care clinic for yet another ear infection. What she believed would be an appointment ending with the prescription of pink bubble gum antibiotics soon became an appointment that altered the course of our lives drastically.

"Has anyone talked to you about her heart murmur?" the urgent care doctor casually asked.

He had no idea about the weight of that one simple question.

My mom has trouble remembering the rest of that specific

appointment. I'm assuming my simple and *oh-so-normal* ear infection became an insignificant part of the conversation that day.

I was supposed to be Blaine and Julie's miracle child. I was supposed to be different from Rachel. I was supposed to be *normal*—but I wasn't. In fact, we soon found out that I have the exact same heart defects that Rachel had.

My parents would eventually have two more daughters. My sister Linsey was born two and a half years after me. She was finally the healthy child they had prayed for. And two and a half years after Linsey, my sister Taryn arrived strong and healthy. Four girls: two healthy, one gone, and me—*the broken one.*

As a very young child, I became familiar with EKGs and echocardiograms. Until I was trained and old enough to understand the procedures, my doctors would use restraints to keep me still for exams that were necessary to monitor my condition. My poor mama. As I got a little older, the exam technicians started offering Disney VHS movies on a big box TV wheeled in on a cart. The movie distracted me just enough to help me lie still and let the technician do his job. I always felt a bit cheated, though, because the echocardiogram exam lasted just over an hour, so I never reached the end of my movie. And they wouldn't let me stay and finish either. I asked. I also have early memories of soaking in the bathtub for hours, trying desperately to gently remove the EKG leads from all over my body. They used to make the leads with cartoon zoo animals on them, so naturally I started a collection. Yes, it's a strange collection, but I didn't know any different. This was my normal.

And I vividly remember one specific appointment occurring when I was seven years old. It changed my life.

I completed my EKG, echo, and other exams as I always did. I watched the typical three-quarters of a Disney movie and sat on the exam table, picking at the leads still stuck to my body while we waited for the doctor. I sat on the crinkling paper in the small, beige room, thinking about what flavor of ice cream I would be ordering after we finally busted out of there. Any parent with a child seeing the doctor regularly understands that ice cream is automatically written into the contract. Finally, when the doctor came in, he brought visuals and diagrams—never a good sign. I don't remember all the details, but I remember my mother trying to look strong for me. I was old enough to know something was different today. My ice cream flavor was quickly forgotten.

After an endless conversation with the cardiologist, my mom and I walked out to the parking lot to find our old, rundown, full-sized van. I hated that van, but in that moment, I had never been so relieved to see it. We climbed in and cried. Both of us. We sat in the van for a long time. This appointment was different from the lifetime of appointments I'd had.

I needed open-heart surgery.

The surgery was quickly scheduled for exactly one week after my eighth birthday. My parents tried to make my birthday extra special and intentionally distracting. We invited a van full of giggly seven- and eight-year-old girls to have the coveted first *real* slumber party. To make it even more exciting, my parents drove us the hour out of town to my aunt's tiny mountain cabin for the night. I had hit the jackpot when it came to eight-year-old birthday parties! But it still wasn't distracting enough from what was coming. I spent the evening hiding in the cabin loft and crying. No amount of sweets, presents, and friends could distract me from the fact that I was about to have my chest cracked open. That was just too much weight to carry.

Over the next week, we prepared for what was rapidly and inevitably coming. My mom and Grandpa Mack donated blood for my operation; we would later find out they were the wrong blood type. My dad wrapped up items at work to prepare for the time off. My sister Linsey, in true middle-child fashion, decided this was the best time to break her arm. In her defense, I did dare her to jump from her bed to our fort constructed of wooden chairs and blankets. You live and you learn. And my Grandma Jackie took me to the toy store at the local mall, where I got to choose any stuffed animal I wanted to go to the hospital with me. It was a quite lengthy and difficult process to make a decision, but I finally picked the softest and least fierce-looking tiger I had ever seen. He was perfect for the job. We were busy and scared and anxious. It was like driving down the road knowing you were about to crash and you couldn't prevent it: everyone was tense.

The day finally came to check in to the hospital. My memory is patchy through this part of the story, but I remember sitting on the anesthesiologist's knee and breathing in the strawberry air; it smelled deceptively sweet and innocent. Then I fell asleep.

Once I was wheeled into the operating room, my mom no longer had a reason to keep on her brave face. She was found in a fetal position on the hospital floor. Fear can be overwhelming, gripping, and ultimately crippling. My mom had transported herself back to the day when Rachel had died on the operating table during open-heart surgery. She was living this nightmare all over again, just with a different daughter.

We will never understand why Rachel was stolen from our family or why I was born with the same birth defects. In the midst of tragedy, people often ask, "*Why* would God do this?" They also ask, "How could He *let* this happen?" The reality is we are not always meant to understand. We are not on the same playing field as God. We do not see what He sees or know what He knows. So how could we possibly know better than He does? We must accept that we are not designed to fully understand, but we are meant to hold onto the fact that God is good *even* when life does not feel good.

This is where my story takes a different turn from Rachel's: my open-heart surgery was successful. My story did not end on the operating table that day. I woke up feeling more broken than whole, but I woke up.

I opened my eyes in the ICU and started my painful road to recovery. It turned out that the surgeon who had been scheduled to perform my surgery had been called to an emergency right before my operation, so I had a last-minute replacement. He was good at his job, but like many surgeons, his people skills were quite lacking. In fact, I think I could safely say he had the worst bedside manner of any doctor in the history of medicine.

After struggling through the initial reentry, my parents knew I was finally feeling better when my first order off the hospital menu was a steak. I was a forty-pound, three-and-a-half-foot-tall, eight-year-old ordering the steak. The nurse chuckled, but I was quite satisfied with my order.

Over the next few days, I had several visitors and enjoyed showing off how I could use my own hospital wheelchair—I was less pleased when I rolled backward down the ramp in the hallway. I memorized my "I Spy" books, filled up my coloring sheets and continued to order steak and pancakes off the menu.

Three days after the surgery, my pediatric cardiologist came to discharge me from the hospital. Upon my smiling departure, he asked me the name of my faithful sidekick, the fearless tiger who had bravely followed me into the operating room and stood guard by my hospital bed every moment since. I had named him Dave—yes, I know, a bit of an odd choice for a little girl to choose for her fluffy tiger with the stitched smile, but that is exactly what I picked—Dave. It was the name of the man who in that week literally helped saved my life—my pediatric cardiologist, Dr. Dave. As an adult I still call him that. I didn't even know his last name until a few years ago.

I was not the same person leaving the hospital as I had been when entering it a few days earlier. My heart now looked different, my body looked different, and my life looked different. Little did I know the recovery was just beginning.

I exited the hospital in my brightly colored Disney pajamas and tiny, pale-pink bathrobe. I had picked out this cozy uniform specifically for this moment, and even though I had more of a postsurgery shuffle than strut, I felt victorious.

"Well, where would you like to eat on our way home? We can stop *anywhere* you want." My mom asked me this question with a tired and relieved smile. With zero hesitation, I answered, "Elmer's." I had no doubt in my mind that the old-fashioned breakfast diner was exactly the place for my celebration meal. Nothing said victory more than a giant plate of golden waffle topped with a mound of strawberries and a tower of whipped cream—I had pretty classy taste.

We arrived at Elmer's Diner, and my mom parked in the handicapped space in the almost-empty parking lot. I was completely appalled. As the oldest child, I'm a *bit* of a rule follower, and for a second grader, parking in the handicap parking space without a legally approved pass was the ultimate crime. We were basically criminals now. I immediately protested being an accomplice to this outright rule breaking, but my mom explained that since I could barely walk it would be ok—*just this once*. I sat in my seat still buckled in and thought this through.

She was right: my shuffle was far from impressive, or quick, for that matter. I needed that door to be close if I was ever going to get my waffle and tower of whipped cream. I unbuckled and stepped out of the car and straight into a life of crime. There was no turning back now, so I straightened the ties on my fluffy pink bathrobe and shuffled the few steps to the door. The waffle was worth it.

After our victory meal, we arrived home to balloons and flowers. I felt special, but I was drained. We lived in an old, blue, two-story home. My sisters and I shared bedrooms upstairs, but we quickly realized the stairs were just not going to work for my current condition. We set up my new camp in the downstairs living room with the hide-a-bed couch. I settled into my new bed and quickly fell asleep. Talk about a long week.

At 5:34 a.m., the earthquake hit. Seriously, an actual, literal earthquake hit our quiet state of Oregon. This *never* happens. I could hear things falling off the walls in the kitchen and hear things breaking as they crashed to the floor. It took me a minute to realize what in the world was happening and where I even was—did I mention it had been a long week? That's when my mom came frantically running into the living room, screaming to my dad who was sleeping upstairs with my sisters, "Is it *under* a doorway? Or *out* of the doorways?"

Natural disasters are not really her thing. I could hear my dad yelling in response, "*Under* a doorway! Under a doorway!"

So naturally my mom hears, "*Out* of the doorway!" Even as an eight-year-old, it was obvious that we were wildly unprepared for this type of situation.

Having no idea where to go or what to do, my mom threw me under the bed. It was a nice thought except for the fact that my chest had literally just been cracked open earlier that week. So there I was riding out the "spring break quake" under the bed, completely unable to move from the pain.

Once the shaking stopped my dad ran downstairs, still in his tighty-whities to check on the safety—and more likely the sanity—of my mom and me. Luckily it was just a hide-a-bed I was under because my parents had to lift the bed to get me out from under it. Not one of my finer moments in life but definitely one of the most memorable. Seriously, an earthquake in Oregon!

The next week was a dark one for me. No one warns you about the depression that follows major surgery, especially in kids. My parents had a bedroom closet that had two sliding, full-size mirror doors. I stood in front of those mirrors and tediously studied my new body. My scar was *brutal*. It was huge and jagged and angry. It ran from my sternum to just above my bellybutton. To make it even worse, the surgeons had used a type of glue over the top of the wound to keep it sealed up and that bloody dried-up glue now had to peel off. I cried a lot and drew sad pictures that scared my poor helpless mom. I felt like a monster.

Eventually the darkness faded and finally lifted, but it would be a long road of learning to love my new reality. I went back to second grade where I had to wear an oversized, bright-red T-shirt that read "Ouch! No hugs please!" and I brought my echo scans for show-and-tell. In those moments, I felt special rather than just *abnormal*.

Over the years, I struggled with being different from other kids, and that destructive self-image took a long time to break free from. In my first year of high school, I refused to wear a V-necked shirt or dress at the risk of someone seeing the top part of my scar. I feared that someone would see that I was different. It wasn't until later that I realized that my scar was not something to be ashamed of and something to hide, but rather it was and is a badge of honor. It is because of that very scar that I am still alive today. Yes, my scar has faded over the years. It is no longer angry and purple, but more than anything, it is my outlook that has changed.

I am a child of God. You are a child of God. He created us in His image. He designed each one of us perfectly. We are "fearfully and wonderfully made." I don't believe that our all-powerful and abundantly creative God who perfectly crafted the entire universe in six days makes mistakes—so if I believe that to be true, it also means that I believe that God created me *exactly* how he intended. I am not a mistake. I may not understand it all, but I can have peace in God's plan for me.

I have learned not to underestimate the beauty of my brokenness. It is through my brokenness that God's glory gets to shine through. It is through my brokenness that the living water runs out to those around me. Only Jesus can use our brokenness for beauty and victory, and only He can make us complete. It is time to shift our views of our brokenness. We need to stop striving for Pinterest-worthy perfection and understand that it will never bring the joy we think it will. Only Christ can do that.

When a person receives Jesus Christ as Lord and Savior, that person enters into an all-sufficient relationship with an all-sufficient Christ. The first line of 2 Corinthians 12:9 (NIV) says, "But he said to me, 'My grace is sufficient for you, for my power is made perfect in weakness.'"

Did you catch that? In weakness! It is through our brokenness that His power is made perfect. The definition of *grace* is "the freely given and unmerited favor and love of God." Unmerited—meaning we don't deserve it and we can't earn it by being *enough*. Let's stop driving ourselves crazy striving to be perfect, stop pretending life isn't messy or full of scars, and stop running from our brokenness. We will never be enough on our own, so we need to stop putting that pressure on ourselves—only He is enough and in Him we are *complete*.

Second Corinthians 12:9–10 (NIV) goes on to say, "Therefore I will boast all the more gladly about my weaknesses, so that Christ's power may rest on me. That is why, for Christ's sake, I delight in weaknesses, in insults, in hardships, in persecutions, in difficulties. For when I am weak, then I am strong."

Life is hard. No, strike that. It's brutal. We all have brokenness in one form or another. Most people, if they are honest with themselves, hope and dream for an easy and simple life, but there is a problem with that. It is because of my trials and hardships—the situations everyone tries to avoid through life—that I had the privilege of learning at a young age that I *need* Jesus. I may not understand all of God's plan for my story, but I can now have peace that I am made complete in Him. There is beauty in the brokenness because it all leads us back to our Savior.

Chapter 1 of my story is important because it was in and through my early battles and brokenness that I discovered I was not created to be perfect and whole and strong on my own—I was created to *desperately* need and cling to Jesus.

And so were you.

I am not the hero of this story. I am the rescued.

2 TALKING IN THE QUIET

After my heart surgery, life went on. I continued to see the cardiologist regularly, but no additional major operations would be needed for several years. I went to school, played competitive sports, performed in the local theater, and I even completed marathons with my dad. My broken heart didn't hold me back one bit.

I graduated as valedictorian from high school, and for the first time, I was truly grateful for my heart condition. It was a compelling scholarship essay topic, and I was soon off to an almost free ride to college.

My first year of school, I went to a state university where I earned my associate's degree in one year. I was on the hamster wheel of striving and searching, so after my first year, I decided to transfer to a college back east. I packed up my bags, and I moved to New York where I went to college on academic scholarship and worked as a nanny.

So many new things for a small-town girl from the Northwest.

I lived in a dorm apartment with three spirited Dominican girls. I listened to a lot of very loud, upbeat Latin music, discovered I liked fried plantains, and was quickly informed that my clunky, brown boots did not belong in New York. They asked me if the Great Northwest was still *wild and scary*, and after I snorted with laughter, I realized the question was genuine.

People regularly gave me the blank stare after I told them I was from Oregon, so I began following it up with "It's right above California." Either that finally connected the dots for them, or I just got the confused response "I thought Washington was above California?" Yes, but there is an *entire* state in between. When a speech assignment came up in my communications class, I sarcastically spoke about the location of my home state. I got an A on the assignment and praise from my professor for my humor, but I didn't build any lasting friendships in that particular class. Oh well, they wouldn't know how to visit me anyway.

I stayed in New York for one school year. It was an adventure, but it wasn't home.

That summer I returned to Oregon. I sold my beloved little black Volkswagen Jetta and used the money to backpack through Europe with my younger sister Linsey. I had just turned twenty, and Linsey was seventeen years old. Now I understand why my poor mother was having anxiety attacks every time we discussed our travel plans.

We went to the local REI and bought our matching Northface backpacks (mine was red, Linsey's was blue), we ordered our Eurail passes and our economy plane tickets, and then we left for the summer. We managed to pack everything we needed into our individual backpacks and also managed to keep them in the carry-on size category. We couldn't risk lost luggage.

We flew out of Seattle to Vancouver, BC, where we were unexpectedly delayed in the airport for eight hours. Since this was in the pre-smartphone era, we had to find a payphone and use our prepaid international calling cards to check in with our parents—not the best system when the entire conversation could be wrapped up in a three-word text message—*"Still* in Canada."

Finally, we boarded the plane that had either been replaced or repaired in the prior eight hours and jetted off to London. I had the middle seat of the middle aisle—lovely.

Before we left, we gave our parents the tentative schedule and planned route. We also discussed that our plan was to stay in a location until we wanted to leave. This strategy kept our visit in France short and extended our adventure in Ireland. Since we were college students traveling on a very tight budget, we would mainly sleep in student hostels, or if we could find an overnight train to a new city that we found interesting, then we would sleep on the train and save the hostel fee.

Over the next two months we traveled through thirteen countries. We flew from Canada to the United Kingdom. Once we arrived, we immediately traveled on the Chunnel to Belgium. From Belgium we rode the Eurail to the Netherlands, to Germany, to Austria, to Switzerland, to Italy, to the Vatican, to Monaco, to France, to Spain, and then back to France where we boarded a ferry boat to cross the English Channel to Ireland. After Ireland, we took a twenty-dollar hopper plane back to London and then finally returned home.

We quickly realized that we could afford about two meals a

day—and one gelato each day while in Italy. We snacked on gritty power bars to tide us over between meals and purchased most of our food at local grocery stores rather than restaurants. It wasn't very glamorous, but it was a true adventure.

We marveled at Van Gogh's artwork in the Netherlands; we ate massive pretzels in the famous Hofbrahaus in Munich; we left the Dachau concentration camp memorial in Germany feeling incredibly humbled; we rode bikes through the streets of Vienna; we sat in awe of the Swiss Alps—God truly is an artist; we got elbowed all the way through the Sistine Chapel tour by Asian tourist groups; we ate the best pizza I've ever tasted in Pisa; we got lost in Venice; we cried as "God Bless America" played over the loudspeakers at Omaha Beach; and we had almost no trouble at all until we reached Barcelona.

We arrived in Barcelona after we had been traveling for several weeks, and we were ready to stay in one city for a few days. We decided to splurge and pay for a private room at the hostel instead of just staying in a regular bunk room. The room was small and sparse, but it was private. We had two twin beds and even a window. But more importantly, we had a bedroom door that locked. We could leave our bags, money, and passports safely behind while we went out. We could even go to the beach now!

On our first full day in Barcelona, we decided to go buy swimsuits and just relax at the coast for a while. We went from shop to shop and found several bikini bottoms, but we had difficulty finding a single bikini top. We realized the reason for our struggle once we actually got to the beach. After we had found *all* the appropriate swim gear needed, we spent the day soaking up the sun and playing in the Mediterranean Sea. It wasn't until we left the beach that we realized that Linsey was *literally* soaking up the sun. She'd forgotten to reapply sunscreen after going into the water, and her pasty white skin was now very, very *angry*.

We found a small grocery store and started searching for aloe vera to put on her already blistered shoulders. I had taken Spanish class all through high school and a year in college, so I could fumble my way through reading basic signs and speaking with locals.

"I found it!" I shouted in victory as I held up the green bottle to show Linsey.

"That doesn't look right," Linsey skeptically said staring at the bottle as we stood in the middle of the narrow aisle.

I was correct. I had in fact found aloe vera. But Linsey was *also* correct. The current bottle I was proclaiming my victory over was spray-on deodorant *with* aloe vera in it—my mistake. I justified the whole incident by reminding Linsey that we realized the error before actually buying it and covering her in spray-on deodorant. We eventually found real aloe vera. We made sure to double-check it before making our purchase. We also bought a small fan for our room because it was the middle of summer in Spain, and even though we thought our private hostel room was a poor student's haven, it was far from luxury and, therefore, had no air conditioning in sight.

Once we got back to our room, we soaked Linsey in aloe vera, gave her some Tylenol, and parked her in front of the small revolving fan. Then we discussed our travel plans because it was very clear that Linsey would not be carrying a pack for at least several days.

We came to the conclusion that we would stay in Barcelona for two or three more days or until Linsey felt better and could carry her backpack.

The next day, we got up and walked around the city for a few hours. On our way back to the room, we made a last-minute decision to grab sandwiches at the little deli on the same block as our hostel. It took only a few extra minutes to run in and get a lunch order to go—but it was those very few minutes that made all the difference.

We leisurely walked the remainder of the block, but as we approached our hostel, we began to notice that something was wrong. As we entered, we heard loud voices, and then we were met with panicked faces. Our entire hostel had just been robbed. The scene we entered was bizarre. Every wood door all the way down the hallway had been smashed to pieces—even the three bathroom doors were hanging on their hinges. Every door except one—every door except *ours*. We had literally missed the incident by moments, and if we had not stopped at the deli for a last-minute lunch, we most likely would have been in the hostel when the invasion took place. I no longer had any desire to eat, but I had also never been so grateful for a simple sandwich!

People began returning to the building and were met with the daunting task of taking inventory of their missing items. Every room was missing jewelry, money, and more importantly, they were missing passports.

Linsey and I shrank quietly back into our room and closed the beautifully solid door.

"Let's just not tell Mom until we get home. I mean, we're completely unharmed, and nothing was stolen, so this news can wait, right?" I asked Linsey in a voice that didn't mask just how shaken I actually was.

"Absolutely! I'm not ready to go home yet." Linsey confidently responded.

So that was the plan—tell mom when we got home. It would be funny by then.

We ended up giving Linsey another dose of Tylenol and packing up early. I carried both of our packs as much as possible, and we picked a train route out of Barcelona.

We left Spain and traveled back to France. Once we arrived in France, we learned we could catch a ferry boat across the English Channel to Cork instead of heading directly back to London where we would fly out to return home in a week. This last-minute change in plans meant we would lose some time in London, but we had no doubt Ireland would absolutely be worth it. The boat ride took two days, and this was the pivotal moment in my life when I discovered I get *intensely* seasick. Linsey, on the other hand, loved the boat and ate scrambled eggs from the boat's restaurant for breakfast. Seriously, scrambled eggs.

After we disembarked the boat, we boarded a train and headed up the coast to Dublin. Ireland was absolute heaven—beautiful scenery, delicious food, and the kindest people I have ever met. Of all the places we traveled and the things we saw, Ireland was my favorite. No competition.

The next morning in Dublin is still vivid in my mind. We woke up in our bunk beds, got dressed, grabbed our day packs and headed to the complimentary breakfast in the hostel lobby. After living on fairly limited meals and gritty power bars this breakfast was pure bliss. I savored my fried eggs, sliced tomatoes, and toast. After we finished our food, we remained at the table to contently sip our coffee and discuss our plans for the day.

It was then that we began to hear murmurs of panic.

On July 7, 2005, the London bombings rocked the world. Four suicide bombers attacked Central London, killing fifty-two people and injuring hundreds more. Central London was exactly where we had originally planned to be that day.

We immediately checked our watches and did the backward count of the time difference with our parents. We would need to wait to make the phone call home until it was morning in Oregon. The key would be timing it perfectly so we didn't call too early, but it was crucial we called before they had a chance to turn on the TV and see the news. It was a very fine line.

After discussing it, we decided we would rather call a bit early in the morning than risk calling too late.

"Hi, Mom! How are you?" I said with the best faked cheeriness I could manage. I couldn't let her sense trouble in my voice before I had time to clear up some important details.

"*Oh!* I'm so glad you called, what a treat!" She squealed back into the phone. Her joy was sincere, so I knew they had not heard the news yet. I took a deep breath before continuing our conversation.

"Okay, so just remember we are in Ireland, okay? Okay, Mom?"

"Wow, you are in Ireland. That's great! How is it there?"

"So you know we are in Ireland, right? We are in Ireland," I repeated.

"Jordyn, yes, I heard you. You are in Ireland."

"Okay, Mom, go turn on the TV now."

And then I waited.

It was completely quiet until I heard the sound of voices coming from the TV and then—

"*Oh my goodness, are you in London!*" She half cried and half shouted into the phone.

"No, Mom, we are in Ireland. Okay, just put Dad on the phone, please. I love you, Mom."

Dad and I talked for a few minutes. We discussed our plans and our safety. I promised to keep them updated more regularly from here on out and reminded them we would be home soon. I told them I loved them and hung up the phone. Then the next person in line for the payphone stepped up and made his phone call to someone he loved.

Almost two weeks later, we were packed up and preparing to head to Heathrow Airport to start our long journey back to the States. We left our hostel and waited at the bus stop in busy Central London. It was loud and crowded, and I felt completely ready to be back home. As the bus approached through traffic, I prepared my pass for a quick boarding process—we didn't have much time to waste to get to the airport. I boarded and squeezed my way onto the standing-room-only vehicle. The doors closed, and I sighed with relief at starting our process home. I relaxed and looked out the bus windows at the crowd on the sidewalk as we began to pull away. I was staring directly into the face of my sister still standing dumbstruck at the bus stop. She had zoned out and missed the bus. My one requirement for this trip was to bring back Linsey, and now here I was on a bus headed to the airport with her lost in downtown London. When I found her, I vowed to kill her for this.

She frantically pointed down the road motioning to show me that another bus was coming up right behind us. She quickly boarded the second bus and planned to follow my bus to our originally planned location. Somehow in London traffic, her bus pulled around my bus and passed us—we were playing a horrible game of leapfrog. In an attempt to right her wrong, she got off at the next stop, thinking my bus would stop there too—it didn't.

Our panicked eyes met as I passed her—and then she started

to run. She bobbed and weaved through the crowd with her blue backpack bouncing the entire way. She was attempting to beat the bus to the next stop so she could board. All I could do was watch her run.

Running was not Linsey's gift. She was more of a swimmer.

At the next stop, I got off the bus. The bus that we *needed* to be on. I stood at the bus stop and waited for Linsey to arrive. When she finally did, we didn't say a word—mainly because she couldn't breathe yet. We waited for the next bus, bought tickets *again*, and headed to the airport.

It was definitely time to go home.

Finally, we boarded our plane and returned safely to Oregon. Our summer adventure was over, but we were headed back to good things. I would be starting my last year of college, and she would be starting her first. One adventure was over, but more were on the way.

For my third and final year of college, I transferred back to a state university. I went from living in a New York apartment filled with Latin music to living in my grandparents' basement while I worked part-time and completed twenty-four credits a term.

I started each day with reading the newspaper and drinking black coffee with my grandpa. Having a twenty-year-old living in the same house did not shake up their routine in the least bit. In fact, I easily fell right into it. You could say I'm a bit of an old soul—boring sounds a bit harsh. As I write this, I'm flooded with overwhelming affection and appreciation for my grandparents. Mack and Jackie started dating when they were fifteen years old and were married almost sixty years, right up until we lost my grandma to cancer in 2012. My grandpa is now in a battle with dementia, and there is no stopping its gripping control. That year living in their basement was an incredible gift. Trading sections of the *Oregonian* with Grandpa while Grandma studied the *TV Guide* magazine on their brown floral davenport—it's usually the simple day-to-day life that we later realize was beautiful. We underestimate the gift of time. Today, take the time to call someone you love and tell them.

Needless to say, my routine was simple and consistent that school year. Five days a week, I would eat my toast and drink coffee with Grandpa, and then I would commute almost an hour into Portland for school. I would drive directly to the parking garage on campus, attend classes back to back from eight to five, and then I would drive back home to study. I didn't get out much.

It was in late spring that things changed.

On May 15, 2006, I drove my typical forty-five minutes south on the highway to attend church in Salem. I loved this church, but I didn't know many people there. I would arrive right before service, sit by myself, praying I wouldn't sit in some elderly woman's "regular seat" and get asked to move—it had actually happened before—and then I would drive back home to my grandparents' house right after the service. This Sunday was different, though. I decided it was time to branch out a bit and attend the young adults class before the regular Sunday service. Maybe I just had the itch to be around people my own for age for an hour or two.

I entered the class, found a seat, and looked straight ahead, waiting for what was to come next. This was not in my comfort zone—not even close. To my horror, the teacher started that morning by asking everyone to find a partner and complete the icebreaker activity. In that moment, I almost bolted. The introvert in me did not approve of this. So I unwillingly looked around for someone in my near vicinity who didn't come with someone or already have a partner.

And that's how I met my husband.

I was paired up with Brian Glaser. The icebreaker assignment was to draw a picture of your pets and then tell the other person about them. Well, poor Brian lived on a farm—his 8x10 paper was completely *full* of the worst stick-figure livestock I have ever seen—visualize a flock of stick-figure sheep for just a moment. I, on the other hand, had two dogs. It was a bit of a lopsided conversation, but it was also the first time I got to laugh with my husband.

That was a good day.

After that Sunday morning in May, we started dating. We were engaged by September, and married in January. I was twenty-one years old, and Brian was barely twenty-two when we got married. We had no idea what we were doing, but we knew we wanted to do life together—little did we know that the next decade together would be full of joy and hardship alike.

This time in my life was about growing, learning, and exploring. In these years, I graduated from college, traveled the world, and got married—all happy occasions, right? I almost didn't write this section of my story into the book because it felt too simple and somewhat uninteresting in the big picture.

But here's the thing—our life goes in seasons, and God wants us in *all* seasons. He does not want us to only go running to Him when things are hard. He does not want us to pray only when we need something. He wants us *all* the time. Just as a parent loves his or her child, He wants to be a part of our daily lives. He wants to be exploring the streets of New York City with me, riding in the small train compartment through Germany by my side, and absolutely holding my arm as I walk down the aisle. He loves us and wants us, and that is *truly* amazing! And even more amazing is that He does not want us because of the things we have done or because of who we are but rather because of what *He* has done and who *He* is. We are loved by an awesome God, and He wants to be in relationship with us no matter what season of life we are in.

John 15:4 (ESV) states, "Abide in me, and I in you. As the branch cannot bear fruit by itself, unless it abides in the vine, neither can you, unless you abide in me."

When Jesus says, "Abide in me," He means a personal relationship and daily walk with Him. Talk to Him. Tell Him about your day— what made you thankful, what made you cry, what are your dreams and your goals—He wants to hear it. He wants to know you! How incredible is it that the God of the universe pursues *us*?

The bottom line is that if you walk alongside God and talk with Him in the quiet, then His voice will be much easier to hear in the heat of the battle.

3

Taking Steps with Fear

Brian and I were married on January 13, 2007. Not a popular time in the Oregon Willamette Valley to get married.

Just as the ceremony music started, I stood at the back of the center aisle, watching through the tall stained glass windows of the church as the snow began to fall. By the end of the short ceremony, the snow was rapidly turning to ice. We rushed through our simple coffee-and-cake reception in the outdated reception hall off the sanctuary and then made our grand exit through a tunnel of tinkling silver bells to our getaway truck. The moment we pulled away from the church parking lot, the guests fled to their vehicles and made the mad dash to get home before the ice completely paralyzed the town.

Our plane flew out for our Hawaiian honeymoon the next day. We later discovered that we were on board one of the last planes to leave the Portland airport before it was shut down due to the massive ice storm that had continued to roll in overnight.

And that was how our marriage began.

About a year into our marriage, Brian shared with me that he had always wanted to be a cop. After that simple confession, we started the process of looking at police agencies and determining which places had job vacancies. As luck would have it, the Oregon State Police was looking to hire new recruits.

The hiring process was long and strenuous. First, he had to pass the physical exams, written exams, and initial background checks. Once he passed the first round, he then went through extensive background checks, home inspection, and psychological testing. The hiring process took almost a year, and in the meantime, I found out I was pregnant with our first child.

Due to my preexisting heart condition, I was immediately sent to the specialist hospital an hour away in Portland. At that point, we were still unclear whether or not my heart defect was genetic, so the doctors wanted to monitor the baby's development throughout the pregnancy—this was not a surprise. I was referred to perinatology (department for high-risk pregnancies) to have an ultrasound when I was thirteen weeks pregnant.

I remember the ultrasound technician's name was Chris. He was kind and smiled as I nervously chattered away on the table. This being my first ultrasound, I was in awe at what I was seeing on the screen, but I didn't understand what I was looking at quite yet. I asked a lot of questions—poor Chris. He took the time to point out different things on the images and was even able to tell us our baby was a little boy—we were going to have a son!

After he was done with the exam, he flipped on the lights and said he would go grab the doctor to review the ultrasound with us. It was then, when I could fully see his face in the light, that I realized he looked worried. Then he closed the door, and we waited.

"Your baby has gastroschisis." The perinatologist seemed to be speaking too quickly. I couldn't keep up with her.

"There is a hole in his abdomen, and his intestines are developing on the outside of his body. We can go into my office and discuss your options."

It took me a long time to process what she was saying, and all I could think was, didn't I see that on a *Grey's Anatomy* episode a few years ago—this is a real thing? Then I felt Brian take my hand and slowly help me walk down the hall to a small room.

It was hard to breathe in there.

"Here's the thing." She continued with no emotion, "You already have a heart condition that is putting you at high risk, and this baby has a major defect, so I would recommend you terminate today."

Wait—what? No, this is not how pregnancy is supposed to happen. This is not what the books talk about. This is not how it goes in the movies.

I finally spoke. It took everything I had. "But my cardiologist cleared me for pregnancy."

"After reviewing your medical history, I don't think your aortic valve is strong enough to withstand pregnancy. Basically, you could die walking up the next flight of stairs." She was so matter of fact.

At that point, she had stopped talking about our baby and was completely focused on the fact that she believed my heart would give out at any moment.

"No," I said quietly but firmly. "I won't abort."

She could see I was firm in my decision, so she turned to Brian, looked him in the eyes and said, "And you? Who are you going to choose? Your wife? Or the baby?"

I remember looking at him in that tiny room with tears in my eyes. This was not how it was supposed to go. I can't remember the words that were said next, but I remember they were heated and emotional. In that moment, we had to fight for our son against what the doctor and the world would tell us. The bottom line was that God did *not* make a mistake, and it was not up to us to decide how and when either of us would leave this world. We were not created to have that kind of control.

I left the hospital that day completely brokenhearted. As we drove home, I sobbed hysterically lying across the back seat of the car until I finally tired out and fell asleep.

When we got home, I put the ultrasound picture on the fridge and placed the magnet directly over the now visually obvious defect. I hadn't seen it before, and now it was all I could see. The magnet covered our son's abdomen so I could focus on the black-and-white profile of his small, beautiful face. He was real. He was mine. And he was worth fighting for.

As I lay on the bed completely empty of tears and energy I thought of the story of Jesus calming the storm. I was in the middle of the fiercest storm of my life, and I was terrified.

> Then he got into the boat and his disciples followed him. Suddenly a furious storm came up on the lake, so that the waves swept over the boat. But Jesus was sleeping. The disciples went and woke him, saying "Lord, save us! We're going to drown!" He replied, "You of little faith, why are you so afraid?" Then he

got up and rebuked the winds and the waves, and
it was completely calm. (Matthew 8:23–26, NIV)

"You of little faith, why are you so afraid?" With these words
running through my head over and over, I realized that while I was
still on the boat, He had control of the storm.

The next evening, we took a walk in the park where we got
engaged. The river bordered the edge of the park, and there were
benches scattered along the walking paths to sit and relax. We found
a quiet spot and sat on the wood bench for a while before either of
us spoke. What do you say when you are twenty-four years old and
discussing the possibility of dying? Where do you even begin?

We left the park bench that night with the intention to fight as
hard as we could for the little life God had entrusted to us. It was
very clear that our initiation into parenthood would not be easy, but
I don't believe God calls us to comfort.

When it came down to the question of fight or flight, we planned
to fight this battle as best we could. We would not listen to the
voices of the world telling us that our son was broken and therefore
unworthy of life. We would not listen when doctors told us to make
the choice. We didn't know what the outcome of the battle would be,
but we fully trusted our leader and planned to hold the line.

I was terrified.

Over the next five months I traveled the one-hour-and-thirteen-
minute commute from our house to Oregon Health and Sciences
University (OHSU) in Portland. On Tuesdays, I went in for an
ultrasound and regular checkup, and on Fridays I went in for fetal
monitoring. We were now working with a new doctor and a team of
people who agreed to support us through this journey. Since we were

all in this together, I made it a part of my routine to bake cookies on Monday nights and bring them to the office for my Tuesday appointments. Cookies always bring joy.

At our appointments, we watched as our son struggled. Each ultrasound the technician measured the intestines to see if they were becoming dilated or, heaven forbid, if the intestines were twisting or even dying off in sections. It was a weekly rollercoaster, a good appointment, a bad appointment, and then more waiting. In the meantime, I was also being monitored by my cardiologist. He had come to the conclusion that while he believed my heart to be strong enough for pregnancy, they would not be taking any risks, so I would be monitored the remainder of the pregnancy.

At home, I struggled with how to prepare for a child who may not come home from the hospital. The idea of setting up a nursery terrified me. What if the crib we spent hours building would never be slept in, the baby bath never used, the toys never played with? The memory of my dad telling me about Rachel's empty room and the lingering smell of baby powder kept circling through my head.

Then came the moment when I realized I was more determined to *fight* for my baby than fear for him, so I told my poor, patient husband that we needed a nursery, and we needed it *now*. We spent weeks painting, building, decorating, and strolling the aisles of Babies 'R' Us, collecting all the "essential" items needed for your first baby. It was like a therapy for me. I had crossed over a line, and there was no going back. I had reached a point where I would stop saying "if" and I would start saying "when." *When* my little boy came home from the hospital, he now would have a beautiful room of his own.

Finally, at thirty-six weeks, I went in for my regular ultrasound, but this appointment was different. I could read the fuzzy ultrasound screen and the technician's poker face fairly well by this point, and I knew something was wrong. The intestines were measuring too wide. They were becoming too dilated and were in danger of permanent damage. It also appeared that his stomach and bladder were now being pulled and at risk for coming out of his tiny body as well. The technician finished the ultrasound, and the doctor came in to tell me what I already knew—our son would be born today.

Brian was sent out to the parking lot to make calls and to retrieve our bags from the car. I was delicately placed in a wheelchair and whisked off to the labor-and-delivery unit.

Most women make detailed birth plans—a Jacuzzi tub, a ball to bounce on, strolling the halls, diffusing oils, a music playlist. This was not my experience. I was taken to the room at the end of the hall, the room closest to the resuscitation room. I was immediately hooked up to more machines than I knew existed. Labor was induced, and then we waited for the excitement to begin.

Labor was difficult to get started because I was only thirty-six weeks along. My body was just not ready and needed a lot of encouragement. My Pitocin dosage kept increasing and other measures were taken that we won't discuss in this book so I can keep some degree of modesty.

As if I weren't already hooked up to enough machines, the cardiologist and perinatologist had decided that due to my heart condition and our son's condition, I needed to have an epidural put in but *not* activated. Such a cruel joke. The logic behind this decision was that if things turned dangerous for our son during the delivery, the team would activate the epidural and operate to get him out. The downside being that an epidural lowers heart rate and they didn't want to risk that with my heart.

After hours of contractions and slow progress, the doctor decided to break my water because our son's heart rate was dropping and we needed to move things along. The doctor performed the quick and painless procedure and promised to come back in four hours to check my progress.

She paused in the doorway, turned, and said, "We have had a team of students on the delivery floor all day, and they have yet to see a natural delivery. All the deliveries today have been C-sections. Would you mind if they come in to observe the delivery? That is, if baby is born before they are done with their shift later tonight?"

OHSU is a good teaching hospital, and frankly, I was a fascinating case. I looked around my hospital room, trying to visualize what the delivery might be like. I would have the delivery team, the cardiology team, the NICU team, and now a gaggle of students. Talk about losing all modesty.

"Sure, if they can find somewhere to stand in the back, then they are welcome to observe."

She chuckled at the truth of that comment and then again promised to see me a few hours before she left.

Thirty minutes later, I was pushing the Call Nurse button.

The nurse came down, took one look at me, and set off all the alarms in the hall. I was *that* patient. The patient who makes the staff run. The one whom all the other patients who are quietly resting in their rooms look to their loved one and say, "Ooh, I wonder what is going on?" That was me.

All 35,001 doctors, nurses, and students came rushing through the door and began to prep and take their places for the best viewing.

I gave one and a half pushes, and our son Davis entered the world. And just like that, the doctor wrapped him up and swiftly left the room with my newborn son. I didn't even get to see him.

Brian and I had worked out ahead of time that he would go with Davis into the resuscitation room for the operation, and my mom would come into the delivery room and stay with me. After Brian and Davis left the room, I cried while my mom held my hand. The physical pain was nothing compared to the emotional pain. I was scared and overwhelmed.

I was a mother with no baby to hold.

A well-meaning nurse who had just been added to my team saw my discomfort and the fact that I was hooked up to the epidural and said, "Oh here, honey, just press the button to help your pain level."

And then she hit the button to activate the epidural.

I had just labored and delivered my baby with literally zero medication, and now I was laying in my hospital bed with my legs going numb. I was extremely unhappy.

Davis's procedure went smoothly, and there were no complications. His intestines had not tangled or twisted, and there were no signs of damage. The swelling was minimal, and the surgeon concluded that he could put everything back in with one repair. Some babies with gastroschisis require a "silo" a procedure in which the doctors put the intestines in a sterile bag and hang them above the baby's sedated body and slowly squeeze the organs back into the body over days or weeks. I had been praying against a silo since the day we learned of the method, and I was incredibly grateful for the answered prayer.

By the time Davis had been born his bladder had also come out of his body cavity. Our now eight-year-old Davis still loves the story of how the surgeon tested Davis's bladder by giving it a small squeeze and a stream of urine shot out all over the operating table—what is it about boys and bathroom humor? After the surgeon put everything back inside Davis's tiny body, he sealed up the opening with a portion of the umbilical cord and bandaged it up neatly as if the problem had been minor and unsubstantial.

On the other side of the hall, the doctors were finally satisfied with my condition, and I was unhooked from my machines. I was told that Davis was all done with his surgery, and I could go see him in the resuscitation room. I could finally see my baby for the first time. Since my legs were still fairly useless from the helpful nurse, Brian assisted me into a wheelchair and wheeled me across the hall to go see our son.

As Brian slowly pushed me into the room, all the nurses stepped back from the tiny hospital bed and watched me. I think I, along with everyone else, was holding my breath.

I could now look at the little life I had fought so hard for. He was real, and he was mine.

Since Davis was sedated and hooked up to multiple machines to make his fragile body work, I wasn't allowed to hold him. That special moment, a privilege that most take for granted, would have to wait a few days. It was painful. I rubbed his small hand with mine and whispered to him that I loved him and I was so happy he was finally here. And then my time was up, Davis had to be taken to the NICU for more observation before we could be with him again. And then I was slowly wheeled back to my empty hospital room away from my baby.

Davis was born at 7:12 p.m., so by the time he was settled into the NICU, it was late, and the doctors explained to us that we could visit him in the morning. The morning could not come quickly enough for me. Mothers are not meant to be separated from their babies. We are just not designed that way.

When morning finally came, I half shuffled, half ran down to the NICU in my sweat pants, purple hoodie, and slippers. We were buzzed into the locked unit and coached through the sign-in security process and the wash station. The babies in this unit were fighting for their lives, some more than others, and it was crucial to protect them from outside illness. On every visit, we scrubbed up to our elbows with hospital-grade antibacterial soap *twice* while using foot pedals to operate the soap and water. The smell of that soap still transports me back to the NICU every time.

The NICU at Doernbecher Children's Hospital is an open unit. It is broken down into "pods" constructed of three walls opening into the main hallway. Each pod holds four baby beds (one in each corner), the nurse's station in the middle, and a wooden rocking chair next to each bed. It was not private or comfortable.

As I finally approached Davis in his hospital bed surrounded by machines that were keeping him alive, I saw how fragile he was, and I cried. I cried for my struggling baby boy, I cried because of the overwhelming fear and exhaustion, and I cried for the loss of a dream of a healthy baby. I grieved for the experience I thought I would have. I couldn't even hold my own child.

Finally, on day three of life, we were told Davis was coming off the ventilator and that we would be able to hold our son. I sat in the wooden rocking chair next to his bed, and the NICU nurse and Brian coordinated lifting Davis out of the bed while keeping all of his IV lines and monitors untangled.

He was absolutely amazing.

I studied him and was so completely in love. He had strawberry hair and dark almost black eyes. He was delivered quickly, so he had no swelling or puffiness. But after a moment, I chuckled and looked up at Brian,

"He has quite the haircut," I said, pointing out the fact that the surgical team had shaved *half* of Davis's head to insert an IV line and secure it with a square patch of tape. It is good a thing newborns normally have awkward hair.

Our time in the NICU became our normal life over the next month. I was discharged from the maternity ward after a day, and we moved into the Ronald McDonald House on the campus.

The unit shut down for one hour from 7:00 to 8:00 a.m. and again from 7:00 to 8:00 p.m. for shift changes. Other than those time frames, I became a constant fixture in the unit. I didn't want to miss anything. I kept telling all the well-meaning people who were concerned for me that if I had a healthy newborn, I wouldn't just drop him off at someone's house and say, "Well, just let me know how he does." I was his mother, and I needed to be with him.

As you can imagine, the body takes an adjustment period when it develops incorrectly and then is put back together. Davis couldn't eat anything until we knew that things would move through his tiny system. He had a tube running through his nose down to his belly to release bile that didn't pass through properly. Until that stopped happening, he couldn't eat. It is still one of the most difficult things I've ever experienced to sit with my tiny hungry baby and not be able to feed him. It was also very physically painful because I spent every waking hour in a room literally filled with crying babies, and God, being the amazing creator He is, designed a mother's body to respond.

After a week or two Davis's organs began to work, and we were given permission to start feedings. This process was a fine dance of two steps forward, one step back. His feedings began with dipping a Q-tip in milk and then rubbing it in his mouth—that was a feeding. *If* his body tolerated that after a few feedings, then we would move up to two milliliters. With two milliliters, we didn't use a bottle, just a dropper. After two milliliters, we went up to five milliliters—and then his body rejected it and we started over. We did this every day with the goal of being able to remove all of his tubes and letting his body work on its own. It was frustrating.

We spent the Thanksgiving holiday at the hospital, and thoughtful volunteers brought a Thanksgiving meal to the Ronald McDonald House so it would feel a bit more like home. It helped and hurt all at the same time. We just wanted to be home as a family.

After a month in the NICU, Davis was cleared to be released! It was freeing and terrifying. I was a first-time mom taking home a fragile baby. I had become addicted to the monitors, studying every stat as it jumped up and down, watching the steady rhythm of his heartbeat—I questioned my ability to know the signs of distress without them. What if I missed something? How would I know what was going on in his body? I genuinely wondered how mothers with healthy babies could just casually leave the hospital after one day. It was overwhelming.

We said goodbye to all the staff, the people who had loved and cared for our son over the last month, and then we loaded him into our small car and headed home. The ride was just over an hour, so naturally Davis had a blowout in his car seat, and we had to pull over to change his diaper, his clothes (and then my clothes), and wipe down the car seat. This was real-life parenting.

Then we were home. The moment we had waited for. We walked in and immediately looked at one another—something was wrong.

It was winter, and we had turned the heat down while we were gone, but this was *too* cold. We looked at the thermostat, and it was a cool crisp fifty degrees. The furnace was broken.

Our big homecoming moment was not what we had planned. We loaded Davis and his mountains of baby gear back into the car and then drove down the street to our close friend Dallas's house. Brian went to high school with Dallas, and they'd remained best friends because they had a guy's understanding of how friendship works—spend time together when they can, probably no phone calls or conversation in between, and yet pick up where they left off last time. They were true friends, and right now we were grateful that we could just walk into his very little and very *warm* home.

Brian and Dallas chatted about the furnace. I didn't care to listen because frankly I just didn't care about the details. I just wanted heat quickly. Somehow over the next few hours, they made some calls and picked up some parts, and the furnace was functioning. It would need more attention soon, but right now, they had it limping along enough to warm our house.

Now we were finally home.

We quickly settled into our new normal at home. Davis was a month old when we were discharged, and Brian had missed a lot of work during our hospital stay. He was still a recruit with the state police, so he needed to get back to work now that we were out of the hospital. He had completed the first portion of his time living at the police academy the month before Davis was born, and Brian was now currently in the "coaching" process. After several weeks of the coaching, he would return to live at the police academy for another four months.

I understood the conditions of Brian's job, but after a few weeks of the long hours he was working, and being a restless first-time mom, I decided to mix up our routine and go visit my parents.

They lived two hours away over the mountain pass. We made the trip without any issues, and we were soon settled into my parents' guest bedroom. It was nice to have some company and someone to hold and bounce Davis when his tummy was bothering him. If you have had a baby with a sensitive tummy, you know just how much you bounce and walk, and bounce and rock, and walk and stroll and bounce. My baby had somehow become my physical trainer, and he was relentless!

After we had been settled for a day, I went into the bedroom to change Davis's diaper. Just as I was laying him down on the changing table, he spit up, but it wasn't the color of normal baby spit up. It was bright green—the same green bile we saw every day in the NICU.

I yelled for my mom, and she came running up the stairs. She took one look at what was going on and grabbed my phone. I called the pediatrician while my mom cleaned up Davis and began the bouncing routine. I hung up the phone and told my mom that we were headed to the ER. This was not the relaxing getaway I had planned.

We drove the thirty minutes to the Bend Emergency Room and waited for a room. It was loud and busy and completely overwhelming.

We were quickly (by emergency room standards) put in a room and the curtain pulled shut. Davis was so small that the ER equipment was basically useless, so the nurse left us alone until the doctor came in. He listened to our history, did a quick exam, and then said, "Anyone smaller than a good-sized salmon shouldn't be treated here. We need to send you back up to OHSU."

I wanted to scream. We had *just* left! We were free! He was supposed to be healthy and normal and better now.

I looked down at the floor trying to breathe and blink the sting out of my eyes. "Okay, that's fine," I said in complete defeat. Whatever it took to get my little boy better again.

The next part was the worst. I held down my screaming terrified infant while the nurses inserted an IV (with an arm bar) and also a tube through his nose into his stomach to relieve the pressure in his abdomen. This wasn't a new procedure for us, but the awful part was that this was not the NICU and therefore not the NICU equipment. Everything was too large for Davis. He struggled and gagged repeatedly on the tube until they finally got it in place and he wore himself out and settled down. In that moment, I felt like doing the same.

Because it was January and a winter storm had blown into the area, the hospital decided that flying us in the Life Flight helicopter wouldn't be safe and that we needed to travel in a small plane. Davis was placed in his car seat carrier, and it was strapped to a gurney. The EMTs then wheeled out my tiny fragile son to the ambulance for transport.

We drove to the airstrip where we were loaded into a small plane. The gurney was loaded, and then two EMTs and I boarded and prepared for the flight to Portland. It was a fairly quick flight—I think. The EMT across from me did a good job of keeping me calm. I always wish I could have gone back and told him what a difference he made. We landed and were transported again by ambulance to OHSU.

We were back.

I had called Brian from the Bend hospital, and he met us in Portland. We were immediately admitted to the pediatric ICU and given a private room to settle in. The nurses quickly tended to Davis and replaced everything with pediatric-sized equipment.

Then we were left in the quiet room to wait.

Over the next week, the surgeons would run every test they could think of, none of which I could explain to Davis. How do you explain to an infant to hold still during a scan, to drink the chalky drink, and to not pull out his tubes? We were all tired and frustrated. Finally, after several days of dead ends, the surgeon with the gift for medicine but extremely poor people skills came to our room and announced without expression that he couldn't find the problem and he, therefore, had come to the conclusion "failure to thrive." And then he left the room. Not helpful.

In one last attempt to find a solution, the medical team decided to take Davis off breast milk, go against everything the books tell you to do, and give him formula. This formula was partially broken down and should be easy on his system.

It was magic!

All of the sudden, he was keeping food down, his poor abdomen was no longer distended and firm, and he was getting better.

All this time his little body had been struggling to digest breast milk, and we had no idea. Every time I fed him, I made it worse. What I thought was providing him with nourishment was actually breaking down and destroying his system.

Once we made the switch to formula, Davis quickly rebounded, and we were discharged from the hospital. This time for good. As we checked out, we were informed by the woman working the desk that we were on the *last* week of Brian's double coverage of medical insurance so we were free to go. It turned out that Brian's previous job had provided an extra four months of coverage upon his exit date, and his new position with the state police had immediate coverage upon his start date—God sure doesn't miss the details. The ER, the ambulance, the flight, the week in the pediatric ICU—it was all covered.

After we left the hospital the final time, our sweet boy began to grow and thrive. He began gaining weight and hitting developmental milestones. His bright strawberry hair grew back where the doctors had shaved it. He quickly developed a love of animals and a hatred of pants. This was the child we were told to abort, to throw away, the child that was not worth the fight. Other than a funny-looking belly button, and honestly what is a *normal* belly button, he was a perfectly healthy and happy little boy.

There was no doubt in my mind that our son was worth the fight. I was exhausted and battle worn, but never for a moment did I doubt that God was in command the entire time. I was scared, but I trusted Him. It is crucial to remember in life that faith is not the *absence* of fear. I guarantee you that Daniel was terrified when he was in the lion's den, but he had faith that God would be there with him, and he took action in faith. Sometimes faith means just taking the first step and then the next and then the next—but the fear may never go away.

I knew I would do it all over again without a second's hesitation if I had to—little did I know that I actually would. As I took off my armor and settled into our life of normalcy, I would soon learn that this was just a time to refuel and regain my strength. Another battle was looming just beyond my range of sight.

4 BUILDING THE FOUNDATION

We quickly fell into stride with our new life as a family of three. We were so in love with our busy and happy little boy. Boys just have a special kind of energy. Davis was a ball of fire and an absolute joy to our family. He was an early mover—and therefore, crasher—and he climbed anything that was stationary.

Shortly after we celebrated Davis's first birthday Brian and I began talking about expanding our family. We had already held lengthy conversations with our doctors about the safety of trying to have more children. The perinatologist explained to us that gastroschisis is *not* a genetic defect and therefore could not happen again. The odds were one in ten thousand, and Davis just happened to be the one. My cardiologist also took the time to run multiple tests and finally gave me the green light for future pregnancies. The conclusion was that while I do in fact have a bad aortic valve, it is strong enough to withstand the extra pressure from pregnancy.

We loved being parents and knew we wanted more children. We also knew several couples around us who were having trouble getting pregnant and that it may also take a while for us as well, so we just needed to be patient and trust God's timing.

A month after that conversation, I was pregnant. We plan, and God laughs.

Shortly after finding out I was pregnant, Brian had to return to complete his last six weeks of training at the police academy. It was not an ideal situation, but it was the reality of the job. As his wife, I understood the importance of him being well trained and well prepared, and this was just part of the sacrifice.

Halfway into his stay at the academy, I was scheduled to go up to OHSU for my initial thirteen-week ultrasound. Even though I had been cleared for pregnancy, I was still considered a high-risk case because of my heart, and therefore, I needed to be seen at the specialist hospital. No one was worried about anything coming up in this exam, so I told Brian I would let him know how it went, and I asked my mom to watch Davis while I went to my appointment alone.

I arrived at the office early, and as was my routine, I had a plate of cookies in hand. It had only been just over a year since I was here for my last pregnancy, so most of the staff was the same, and it was comforting to know faces and names.

I waited for about fifteen minutes until a young and smiling technician opened the door and read my name off her clipboard.

"Hi, there, my name is April, and I will be doing your ultrasound today," she said as she walked me down the hall toward the ultrasound room.

"Hi, April, I'm Jordyn." I said, smiling back at her. It's always a relief to get a technician who is friendly and won't make the next forty-five minutes awkwardly quiet.

We entered the room, and she took her seat in the swivel chair at her station while I climbed up on the table and got comfortable. I was excited and anxious. In the past, ultrasounds had not been a very positive thing for me, but today I was going to get to see my baby, my healthy baby, for the first time.

As April prepped all the equipment, I made small talk to keep things comfortable.

"So how long have you been at OHSU, April?"

Again she smiled as she responded. "Oh I'm a student in my senior year here."

"Wow, good for you. This is a great program," I replied. And I meant it.

Then it was time to get things started. She grabbed the squeeze tube that resembled a ketchup bottle at a small-town deli, except it was clear rather than red, and she squeezed warm gel onto my belly. She grabbed the ultrasound wand and began doing big, sweeping circles across my abdomen to spread the gel. Then she started searching for the first image on her checklist. As she made another move across my belly, I saw a glimpse of my tiny baby, and my breath caught in my chest. April continued to move the wand around, but I couldn't focus.

"Um—did you just see that?" I tried to keep my voice steady and not sound like an emotionally unstable pregnant woman. I continued. "Because I know what I saw, but I need you to tell me." I was starting to lose my composure, and my voice sounded a bit shaky even to me.

April kept her eyes deliberately locked on her screen.

"Well, I've actually never seen that before, and I'm not sure what it is, so I will just get some other measurements ..." She tapered off, still without making eye contact.

I found my voice again and said in a kind but firm tone, "April, I know what that is, and I think you need to go get the doctor now."

April nodded her head in agreement, and as she got up out of her chair to leave, I could now see clearly that she looked shaken as she hurried out of the room.

"*What in the world!*" Those were literally the first words out of the doctor's mouth as he burst into the ultrasound room just moments after April left.

"Yeah, my thoughts exactly," I responded but without any fire to my voice. It was more like the sound of defeat.

The doctor, one I had not worked with before, then picked up the ultrasound wand and placed it back onto my small yet growing belly. We both stared at the fuzzy black-and-white image of my baby who clearly had the intestines growing outside of the tiny body.

It was happening all over again.

The doctors had reassured me that it wasn't possible to happen again. They explained that they had yet to find a single case where a family had two children with gastroschisis. They repeated again and again that it was not a genetic defect and the odds were one in ten thousand. Yet here we were staring at the ultrasound of my *second* child with gastroschisis. *Seriously?*

The doctor finished up a few measurements and captured the images we absolutely needed but kept it quick. He handed me a small white towel to wipe off the gel and stood up to flip on the lights. We made eye contact, but it took a second for either of us to say anything.

"Okay, so now what?" I was the first one to break the silence.

"Well, I already know what you are going to say, but as your doctor I have to give you the option to terminate."

"No," I said quickly and without emotion.

"Okay, so now that we got that out of the way, we can discuss the game plan." Dr. Samuels was young with a warm and comforting personality. He was down-to-earth and personal. I liked Dr. Samuels. If I was going to do this all over again, I was relieved I had him in my corner to help me fight this battle.

We talked about the basics and scheduled my next appointment but kept the meeting simple—there just wasn't much to say this time around. I understood the defect, the risks, the process. As I stood up to leave, I turned and asked, "Is it possible to get a few printouts from the ultrasound? I think I'm going to need some proof when I tell Brian." I chuckled, but I was dead serious. Brian was never going to believe this.

I made it out of the hospital to the large parking garage and somehow had a clear enough head to locate my car. I climbed in and called my mom. I didn't have the energy to discuss details, but I told her enough. I then explained that I would be late getting back home because I needed to go to the police academy and talk to Brian in person.

As I drove, I felt numb. What in the world was happening? We had already fought this fight, we'd already survived a high-risk pregnancy and a sick newborn—this time was supposed to be different. I wanted to have a healthy pregnancy. I wanted to read *What to Expect When You Are Expecting* and not just the last chapter where it describes all the things that could go terribly wrong. I wanted a baby shower without people giving me the sad and worried eyes. I wanted to buy baby clothes without the fear that they wouldn't ever be worn. I just wanted *normal*. Was that really so much to ask?

I took the exit off I-5 toward the police academy and went through the gate to the large facility. I found a parking spot as close to the living quarters entrance as possible because my energy was draining rapidly. I signed in at the front desk, and then I waited in the lobby for Brian to appear. He had no idea what was coming, and I had no idea how to tell him.

He finally arrived, and he gave me a quick kiss hello and a tight hug. It had been several days since we had seen each other because visitors could only come one evening a week. Frankly, it was just plain miserable.

As he stepped back from the hug, his brows furrowed. He saw my face. I don't have much of a poker game.

"What's going on? What's wrong?" Brian quickly but gently questioned.

I truly did not know how to respond, so I held out the ultrasound pictures. He smiled a big proud daddy smile and flipped through them slowly to savor the screenshots of our new little baby. I waited. Anyone who has ever laid eyes on an ultrasound picture knows that it is a *bit* difficult to always know exactly what you are looking at unless you are trained. When he reached the picture of our baby showing the tiny profile of the entire body, including the loops of intestine hovering over the small torso, I stopped him.

I pointed to the picture and said, "This is a profile shot of the face and body. There is the cute nose and the hands and the tiny feet"—I took a breath—"and there are the intestines."

He looked up, but no words escaped his mouth. He looked back down again to see the picture clearly for the first time.

"Yeah." That was all I could manage to say before my eyes began to burn, and I tried to rapidly blink back the tears that were coming.

It took a moment, but then he found his voice.

"You're joking?" he said in a tone that was hopeful, and yet he knew the answer. "Okay, let me go talk to the sergeant. We need to leave campus and talk for a bit. I will see if he will allow us to go to dinner to figure things out."

He grabbed my hand, and we weaved through the sprawling halls and staircases of the training facility. This building was not designed to be inviting. Everything looked the same to me, but Brian knew his way through the empty halls. It was nice to not have to think and just follow. The halls were eerily dark and quiet because it was now late in the evening and the regular office staff had all gone home for the day. We finally reached the last door in the corridor, and Brian gave a short knock.

"Come in" came the firm response.

I can't remember the conversation. I was there but not present. Brian and his sergeant talked for a few minutes, and I recognized the sympathetic look I was now accustomed to receiving. People never really knew what to say. Soon Brian was again pulling me by the hand back through the quiet halls and finally out into the parking lot. We loaded into my car, and Brian drove us to the nearest Mexican restaurant he could find.

We found a booth in the back corner of the brightly colored restaurant. The energetic music played overhead, and it felt conflicting with my mood. We ordered and sat in silence. Neither of us was sure where to start. After a minute of filling the void with chips and salsa, we looked each other in the eye, reached across the table to hold hands, and we prayed together. We knew better than to think we had control of this situation.

Okay, God—this is in your hands, and we trust You—we fully trust You—but oh my goodness, this is hard.

We left that dinner shaken but not defeated. We were headed into battle again.

Once we felt up to the task, we began telling people that we were having another baby and this baby also had gastroschisis. Most people didn't say much because honestly what do you say? Some said they would pray for us, some gave hugs, and many cried. And then there were the people who immediately responded with, "Well, you have already done this before, so I'm sure everything will be completely fine!" As an emotional pregnant woman, this response tested my anger management skills *every single time*. It was the *exact* wrong thing to say.

Yes, we had this before, and it was because of that experience that we knew in detail all the things that could go wrong. In fact, we knew firsthand that we *didn't* know if everything would be completely fine. I wanted to scream or kick someone in the shins—I didn't, just so you know. I wanted to tell people to stop trying to make me feel better and just let me be scared. It is okay to be scared. I was a mother who was terrified for my child. I had zero control of this situation, and it was difficult. Friends, if I can give you one piece of advice—don't try to fix or cover a loved one's pain—just be there. Just love them and walk with them. I didn't know if everything was going to be "okay" by my expectations, but I did know that my baby was in God's hands, and I could rest in that.

Over the next several months, I went to my twice a week appointments with fresh baked cookies in hand. Due to the intestines blocking the view, it took several ultrasounds to finally find out we were having a baby girl. We immediately named her Rory Elizabeth, and from that day forward, we prayed for her by name.

As my due date approached, I was diligent about counting kicks and movement. It was crucial to be paying attention to this detail. Both of my kids were busy in utero, so it made this task relatively easy. All was well until one day the movement abruptly stopped. I called my doctor, and minutes later I was on my way to OHSU for tests. The nurse called me back to an exam room as soon as I arrived. She handed me the blue hospital gown to put on, and as soon as I was dressed, there was a small tap on the door, and Dr. Samuels entered.

"All right. Let's see what's going on." There was no small talk because there was just no need for it at this point.

He placed the ultrasound wand from the portable ultrasound machine on my belly, and I held my breath. I think he did too. There on the small screen was the fuzzy black-and-white picture of Rory and then came the music to my ears—there was her beautiful heartbeat.

I breathed.

Dr. Samuels moved the wand a few times, and on each new position he asked, "Can you feel that?"

"No, I don't feel anything," I answered with a mixture of honesty and confusion.

He continued this process for a few more minutes and then took the wand from my belly and turned on the lights. He handed me a small towel for the gel and then said, "Well, baby has flipped breach, and it appears her new position means you can't feel any of her movement."

Good grief—this child was already giving me trouble. I should have known in that moment that my Rory girl was going to keep me on my toes!

I got dressed and checked out at the front desk. I promised to see them a few short days later at my regular appointment and then headed back home.

A few days later, Rory flipped back into the normal position, and things proceeded as planned over the last several weeks of the pregnancy. We scheduled my induction at the thirty-six-week mark. Gastroschisis babies tend to not thrive in the last month of pregnancy and can even spontaneously pass away without warning, so it is not worth the risk.

Since this was our second baby, we had to make a plan for Davis while we were staying in the NICU for a month or longer. The hospital was over an hour away, so commuting back and forth wasn't really an option, and my mama heart couldn't handle being away from my baby that long either. After a bit of asking around, we discovered that the hospital offered long-term trailer parking in one of the parking lots for families who have extended hospital stays. So we ended up borrowing a fifth-wheel trailer from friends and planned to make that our new home for as long as it took.

The big day finally arrived. I was scheduled to be induced at 8:00 a.m. My parents came to our house to stay with Davis while Brian and I left for the hospital. They would join us later.

The car ride was quiet. We were tired, but even more so we were both anxious and nervous. The sun was just rising, and it was a beautiful summer morning. Normally this would be my favorite time of day, the time when most of the world was still quietly tucked away and all was still. I love early mornings and the anticipation of what God has in store. Today was different, though. I wasn't able to enjoy the stillness as I normally would, but I could feel God's comfort all the same. He was right there with us headed into this battle.

I was greeted with kind and sympathetic smiles from the nursing team. They knew I was coming in this morning, and they knew my story. I returned their hellos with a weak smile and handed them the plate of cookies I had brought. I wanted and frankly needed them in my corner—cookies always help with that. I signed some papers at the desk, and then the nurse escorted me to my room. It was at the opposite end of the hall from where I'd delivered Davis. Otherwise, everything else was the exact same.

I changed into my oh-so flattering hospital gown and crawled into the bed. Over the next hour nurses shuffled in and out checking my stats and prepping me for the induction. After I was hooked up to all my monitors, two nurses came in to start my IV line and Pitocin. They quickly introduced themselves and proceeded to explain that one of the nurses was actually a student and asked if it would be ok for her to administer the IV. Since I'd literally grown up with this hospital, I knew firsthand how skilled the staff was, and I also valued how crucial it was to train them well. I always opted to work with the students and never regretted it—until that day.

Both nurses stood side by side hovered over my right arm and Brian sat on my left side holding my hand. Things seemed to be proceeding fine (I never watch) until all of a sudden I felt like I was fading out—world spinning, lights dimming, strength draining, fading. I had never fainted before, but I think I was headed down that road pretty quickly in that moment. I heard muffled and frantic voices, and I looked Brian in the eyes. He looked worried. Then I closed my eyes.

"Umm, she doesn't seem so good," Brian said, keeping his voice level, but I could hear the concern. There was more frantic chatter from the nurses, and then I clearly remember the lead nurse asking the student to step aside.

The world began to come back to me. My stomach was turning, but the room was returning. I looked at Brian to stay anchored.

"I'm so sorry about that," I heard the nurse say to Brian. "We will be right back to mop the blood off the floor."

After the disastrous IV incident, things mellowed out. In fact, they were too mellow. Labor was progressing at a frustrating pace, especially since I was on clear liquids until after the delivery. I get seriously hangry—I glared at Brian with every meal and snack he ate that day. Eventually he just ate out in the lobby. The entire day slowly ticked by, and before we knew it, it was dark outside, and we still had very little progress. The nurse suggested I try to rest that night because I was going to need my strength, but that felt impossible at the time.

The next morning rolled around, and still we were slowly progressing. It wasn't until around 5:30 p.m. that evening that the doctor decided to break my water and help things move along. I was tired and losing energy with each hour. It had been over thirty-three hours. The doctor promised that things should start soon and he would be back in a few more hours to check on me again.

At about 6:00 p.m., Brian was paging the nurse and telling her it was time. Luckily, with my track record, they believed him, and the entire team came running.

I was in a lot of pain at this point, but as the team assembled and prepared their equipment, I turned to the baby nurse, the same nurse who'd helped deliver Davis less than two years ago, and I quickly said between contractions, "I didn't get to see my son when he was born, so if things are going all right, can you just hold up my baby after she is born, like *Lion King* style or something, so I can see her before you take her away?"

She chuckled at my description but understood what I was saying. I think she saw in my eyes just how much it meant to me, too.

"If I can, I will even do better than that!" She smiled and patted my shoulder in an encouraging way.

At 6:16 p.m., my blue-eyed Rory Elizabeth came into this world with one fast and furious push.

The team had quickly assessed Rory's condition and then placed her lower body up to her armpits into a sterile bag to keep her organs safe. I was still trying to catch my breath when the baby nurse came up next to the bed and handed me my sweet baby girl. This was the moment they write about in the books and the moment women talk about years and years later. This was so much better than *Lion King*!

"We only have a few minutes," the nurse whispered and then stepped back to let Brian and me have a moment with our youngest miracle.

She was perfect, and she was mine. In that moment, my heart grew and made room for this little girl.

Too soon, the nurse was back at the bedside, holding open her hands to take Rory away. I didn't want to let go, but I knew that I didn't have a choice. I gently handed over my baby and watched as the team wheeled her out of the room and headed down to the operating room. The surgeon would let us know once she was out of surgery, informing us that we would be able to see Rory in the morning in the NICU. That was a long time to wait.

We heard late that night that surgery went smoothly and all of her intestines were healthy and able to be placed back inside her body. Again, I thanked God for not having to use the silo.

The morning finally arrived, and Brian and I were at the NICU doors as soon as they gave us the green light. We went through the scrubbing routine and quickly found Rory's pod. We slowly approached the large bed holding the tiny body. She had multiple lines and tubes weaving in and out of her fragile arms, legs, and nose, and a large bandage over her incision site.

For several moments, we just stood there and stared at her, feeling torn between wanting to hold her and not wanting to break her. As I studied her, her color quickly began to shift—pink to gray, gray to blue, blue to purple. The machines surrounding her began beeping and flashing, and the nurse came running over. I stepped aside as she scooped up Rory and began thumping her feet and rubbing her chest. Nothing. No response. We watched in horror as another nurse came running over with the tiniest oxygen bag I had ever seen. She placed the cup over Rory's mouth and began slowly squeezing the bag. We all watched as Rory's tiny chest rose and fell with each squeeze.

Finally, after a few minutes of using the bag, Rory began breathing again—and I did too. Her color came back, and she looked peaceful again. I, on the other hand, was a mess. I was gasping for air, the same air my daughter had just struggled to find. The nurse turned to us and explained that Rory was still coming off the anesthesia from surgery and this was a normal side effect. It did not feel normal. The nurse then advised that we go take a break and get some breakfast and let Rory rest. Leaving your child will never be natural to me, but we did as the nurse told us.

Over the next month, we watched our little girl struggle but make progress. She gained weight and strength, and she even gained the title of "NICU diva" because of how she fired off about ten minutes before her scheduled feeding—every single time. And for those of you who don't know, newborns eat every four hours. She was feisty and demanding, and she was a fighter!

At that time, Davis currently held the record for quickest NICU recovery for gastroschisis babies at our hospital. Until Rory. Rory beat Davis by one day—our first experience with sibling rivalry. When we first learned of Davis's birth defect and we were trying to stay positive about the situation, we said, well, just think of what he will be able to tell all of his little buddies when he is older. I pictured the scene something like this:

> Enter group of awkward grade school boys.
> "Hey guys guess what? I was born with my *guts* on the outside!"
> "Oh man! No way!"
> "So cool!"
> High-fives all around. Davis exits scene with new level of cool-guy swagger.

Well, that little scene came crashing down when we learned about Rory. It is just no longer cool to have a little sister with the exact same story—sorry, buddy.

After about a month in the NICU, we were finally home as a family of four. The only remaining evidence of our journey was now *two* funny-looking little bellybuttons—and if I was honest with myself, a new perspective on life. I couldn't be the same person I had been before. I knew now that I couldn't prevent pain or reroute the storm. There was no escaping or outrunning the battles in life—they *will* come.

In Matthew 7:24–27 (NIV), Jesus shares the parable of the wise and foolish builders:

> "Therefore everyone who hears these words of mine and puts them into practice is like a wise man who built his house on the rock. The rain came down, the streams rose, and the winds blew and beat against that house; yet it did not fall, because it had its foundation on the rock. But everyone who hears these words of mine and does not put them into practice is like a foolish man who built his house on sand. The rain came down, the streams rose, and the winds blew and beat against that house, and it fell with a great crash."

The storm will come. The rain will fall. The waters will rise. And the brutal wind will rattle you.

So where have you built your foundation?

5 Following the Detours

Adoption had always been in the plans for us. Even before we were married, we had discussed adoption and felt the call on our hearts. For us, it was only a matter of God's timing—it was a matter of *when* not *if*. As it turned out, it was not long after Rory was born that God began to stir in our hearts that it was time to start the process.

Rory was about nine months old when I first started researching the idea of adoption. We knew and planned that the adoption process would most likely take a few years, and therefore, we needed to give ourselves plenty of time to be patient and wait for the child God had for us. As I began my internet search, I was soon deep in information about adoption agencies, programs, requirements, fees, timelines, and more. It was so much to wade through.

Late one night after the kids had gone to bed, I sat in our room with all the information packets spread out on our bed. I was feeling completely overwhelmed. How do you choose? Where do you even start? As I sat there cross-legged on our bed, I begged God for clarity, "Lord, what do you want us to do? Please lead us to our child. Please give us clear direction." We couldn't make this decision on our own. We needed God to guide us through this process to our child. And I had complete faith that He would do just that.

After a few months of researching and praying, we decided to submit our application with an agency for the Ethiopia program. We were stoked! In around eighteen months, we would be traveling to Africa to bring home our child.

May 1, 2012, we were officially accepted into the Ethiopian adoption program, and we were now in the process of taking steps toward our child. I have always loved the "May Day" holiday—a day in which people run from home to home, ringing the doorbell and leaving a beautiful basket of flowers on someone's doorstep—*just because*. A beautiful, unexpected blessing not because you asked for it but because you were chosen for it. Just blessed by the gift. After that day, I began to call the little baby we were praying for "Baby May." It seemed right.

May Day was the beginning of the beginning. We had been accepted into the program, but now the real work began. Over the next three to four months, we worked on completing our home study. We completed financial worksheets, background checks, and fingerprints (at the local, state, national, and FBI levels), medical exams, personal biographies, tax information, and more. Once we had gathered all of this information, we were then able to schedule our home visits and interviews with our assigned caseworker. I remember debating (with some degree of panic) if I needed to organize my linen closets and clean the garage before her visit—thankfully, it turned out this wasn't necessary. She toured our home, checked our smoke detectors and fire escape plan, and then conducted hours of questions from our living room couch.

At this point in the process, we also had to include some parameters of the child we hoped to adopt. We felt that we were being called to adopt a healthy baby girl, birth-to-twelve months. Since Rory was our youngest child at this point (and it was a requirement to stay within birth order), it made the most sense to us to adopt a little girl so they would have each other for friendship and also for comfort through the transition. We loved the idea of having two daughters close in age. After this exhausting process, the caseworker then typed up our entire life story using all the information we'd compiled, and once completed we officially had a home study—*cue victory music*.

After our home study was written, we then had to complete our dossier. The dossier is needed for international adoptions. It is the official packet of information that will be sent to the country in which you are adopting from. It includes your home study, medicals, immigration clearance, and so on. On September 20, 2012, we submitted our dossier to Ethiopia, and we were officially added to the waiting list to be matched with our daughter. We were number 136.

And then the truly hard part began.

I thought the paperwork process was difficult, but it was nothing compared to the wait. At least throughout the paperwork you are making forward movement—you are completing steps and making progress. The wait is just that—waiting.

Months went by, and although we received a program update at the end of each month, there just wasn't much to report. We went from number 136 to 132 to 131 to 125 to 123 to 121 to 120 and so on. After several months of this, we began doing the math and realizing that where we were on the waiting list and the number of placements that were happening did not add up to a time frame of 18 months as we had been originally told. But still we waited.

I soothed my waiting heart by making baby quilts and keeping a journal for Baby May. I wanted her to know our full journey to bringing her home, and even more importantly, I wanted her to know how desperately we wanted and prayed for her. Before we even knew her we loved her.

> Dear May,
>
> Today we have officially been on the wait list for one year. I am really hoping you don't wait too much longer to come home. I think about you and pray for you every day. You might not even be born yet, but you are already so loved. We know you are worth waiting for, and we have no doubt that God created you to be our daughter and a part of our family. My heart aches for you, and I hope I can hold you soon. We love you, sweetie, and we will continue to wait for specifically you!
>
> Love,
> Mom

But as time went on, things became more and more uncertain. We were hearing rumors of potential intercountry adoption closure in Ethiopia, and our program seemed to be at a complete standstill. Each month, we received an update stating our projected wait to be matched with our little girl—twelve months, eighteen months, twenty-four months, two years, three years, four years. I was in deep, ongoing conversation with God, asking for direction. What were we supposed to do? We had invested two years and almost twenty thousand dollars into this program so far—now what? Where was our daughter? I didn't understand.

The day after Christmas 2013, we received the email we had been waiting for. Although the program was not technically closed yet, it soon would be, and things would most likely not be moving forward from this point on.

I cried and I prayed. I was not prepared to lose the little girl we had longed and prayed for. I had baby quilts and a stuffed bunny in my closet waiting for her. She was real to me, and I was not prepared to lose her that day.

The next morning, I woke up, and my devotions said, "Do not grow weary and lose heart." Do not lose heart! Again, I prayed and asked God what He wanted us to do. I also went back to the questions we'd asked at the beginning of our adoption journey: Do we believe God is calling us to adopt? Do we believe God has a specific child for us through adoption? Do we believe God has a plan? And the big one—do we trust Him *enough* to walk forward in faith?

After many hours of prayer and conversation, Brian and I decided to call a few other adoption agencies who had programs with Ethiopia and ask them for advice. They were also dealing with the current climate in Ethiopia, but since we were not clients, we felt we might get a more honest picture of the situation.

I looked up the contact information for a few agencies, grabbed my phone, and dialed the first number on my list.

"Hello, this is Tina Matlock," said the energetic voice with the Southern accent.

"Hi, Mrs. Matlock. My name is Jordyn, and I have some questions for you if you have the time." I held my breath. I wanted answers so badly, and I was desperately hoping she held them for me.

"Well, of course! What would you like to know?"

And this was the start of the conversation that changed the course of our adoption and our family. It turned out Mrs. Matlock was the director of the agency and knew *all* the details of every program, every country, and every process. This was a God-ordained phone call. She explained that Ethiopia was in turmoil and the programs were desperately struggling—especially the large programs like the one we were currently in.

"If you want a stable process, you should look at domestic adoption."

What? No, that's not what I wanted, I thought immediately. I was absolutely terrified at the idea of an *open* adoption with a birth family. That was exactly the type of situation that I didn't want. And what about drug and alcohol abuse? No, I wasn't strong enough for domestic adoption. I felt pretty sure domestic adoption was not what I wanted, but I politely asked all the appropriate questions about their program and gathered as much information as I could. Then I thanked Mrs. Matlock and hung up the phone.

And in that moment, I was scared. My plans were rapidly going up in smoke. All that I had planned for and waited for was no longer an option, and the options we were left with terrified me. Again, I was at a point when I needed to let go. I needed to trust that God had a better plan than I did—because the bottom line is that He always does.

Over the next several weeks, I talked to God. My prayer throughout the entire adoption process had been for God to lead us to our daughter by closing the wrong doors and opening the right ones. But suddenly I found myself in a place where the doors I wanted to go through were being slammed in my face, and I didn't like it. This was not how I thought He would answer my prayers, but He definitely *did* answer. He had closed every door but one. And now it was time for us to trust Him enough to walk through the one door left open. The door that terrified me.

In January of 2014, we decided to start over, completely start over—new agency, new program, new home study, new payments, new journey, but same faith in God's goodness. When we began sharing with people around us that we were beginning the process of adopting domestically, we were immediately met with pushback. Yes, it was true that we could have more children biologically (doctors were confident that we would not hit the lottery again), but we were not choosing adoption out of fear or because adoption was a "Plan B." People didn't understand, and frankly our decision did not line up with the reasoning of this world.

We could biologically have more children. We had lost all of our time and finances in the Ethiopia process, and adoption was hard and messy—why would we choose to do this? As I found myself repeatedly justifying our choices, I realized that we did not say yes to adoption and to God with conditions in the agreement. We were fully committed because God asked us to be, and we fully trust Him. He never promised an easy journey, He never promised the outcome we wanted. In fact, He never even promised us a child. He just asked us if we were willing to step out in faith and follow Him. And that was exactly what we planned to do.

Again, we went through the paperwork process, and then we scheduled our home visits. At 4:00 a.m. on the morning our new caseworker was scheduled to visit, *all* of the smoke detectors in our home began screeching at top volume. Nothing makes you fly out of bed faster than ten smoke detectors wailing their distressing song. Brian immediately ran through the house, attempting to discover the cause, and I hustled to the kids' rooms. Our house was far from abundant in square footage, and it was quickly apparent that there was no fire to report.

After we'd finally calmed the kids down and were able to tuck them back into their beds, we looked at each other and knew we would not be falling back to sleep. We grudgingly shuffled downstairs. Without talking, we watched the coffee slowly brew and then began to investigate what had gone wrong. As it turned out, smoke detectors have a ten-year lifespan, and *that day* was the ten-year mark. They were officially retired. So at 8:00 a.m., Brian was in the hardware store parking lot, waiting to buy replacements because at noon our caseworker would be walking through our home, inspecting those very same smoke detectors to confirm they were functioning.

In the end, we made it through the home-study inspection and interviews that day. We felt like we were limping across the finish line but we made it. The home study was done—again.

The next step in the domestic adoption process was to create our profile book. The profile book is the photo book that is sent to each birth mother to enable her to choose a family to match with. This book intimidated me to no end. How in the world do you tell your life story and give a true representation of your family through a simple Shutterfly photo book? This small, simple book held a lot of power. I questioned every word I wrote, every picture I included, and how much I should say or not say. Do I talk about God? Do I talk about the role He plays in our family? Or would that scare a birthmother away? I had to remember that God would lead us to the right birthmother, and I had to believe that she would choose us for who we were—and God was the foundation of our family. In the end, I weaved God and His goodness through our profile book, and I confidently included a Bible verse at the end. It is never beneficial to try to make God small, even if the world tells you otherwise.

April 2014 our profile book was submitted and would be soon in the hands of birth mothers.

Again, we were waiting for our little girl.

A few months went by, and we were still waiting. Each month, we received the list of birth mothers who had reviewed our book and said no. It was discouraging and heartbreaking. And then on June 6, my phone rang. I stared at it for a few beats in confusion. It was our caseworker with our Ethiopian program.

"Hello," I said trying to not sound as confused as I felt.

"Hi Jordyn, this is Jennifer. How are you guys?"

"Why are you calling?" is what I really wanted to say. But I didn't. Instead, I politely made the appropriate amount of small talk after having no communication for over two years, and then I gave the expected pause—okay, now tell me why you're calling.

"Well, I'm calling you today because we've had a case come to us, and it made me think of your family."

"Um, okay." I really didn't know what to say, so I stuck with the minimal requirements of conversation.

"We were given a case with an expectant birth mother here in Oregon who is due with a baby boy very soon. The baby has a complicated heart defect, which is why I immediately thought of you." She paused, but again I didn't know what to say, so she continued to fill the void. "We wanted to contact you to see if you and Brian are interested in being presented as a prospective family? If you're interested, I can send you the file."

Then it actually was my turn to respond. I didn't have an out.

"Wow. Well, obviously, I need to talk to Brian. Can you send us the file to review, and we will call you on Monday with our decision?" My brain felt too full. God, what are you doing with this?

"Sure that sounds great. I will email you the file now."

"Okay, thank you. Also, would we be able to transfer our payments from the Ethiopia program to the domestic program then?" I asked feeling hopeful.

"Oh well—no. This would be an entirely new program." She said this quickly, like ripping off a Band-Aid.

I tried to process the idea of starting a *third* adoption process with a zero percent completion rate. Seriously God, what are you doing? I felt frustrated and confused. I truly did not understand what I was meant to do with this, and I quickly told God exactly that.

After I hung up the phone, I went into my closet, sat on the floor, and cried. Moms with young children learn to use their closets as an emotional safe space. I needed a moment to just feel frustrated. There, sitting on my closet floor, I talked to God. I begged Him for clear direction. I wanted to hear His voice. I needed His guidance.

And then I spent the entire weekend listening for it.

My heart ached for this baby, this baby whose heart was built like mine. The more I prayed, the more I felt like we were not meant to move forward, and again I was frustrated. Why would God bring this case to us if He only intended us to say no? Why would God break my heart over this child? Why would God ask me to say no to a child when He knows I want more than anything to say yes? But no matter my frustration, I knew we were not meant to be the family for this baby.

I called the agency first thing on Monday morning and thanked them for thinking of us but told them that we had decided not to move forward with the case.

My heart hurt, but I knew that this was right.

After I hung up with Jennifer, I immediately called Tina.

"Hi, Tina, this is Jordyn." I was talking fast, but I had a sense of urgency and purpose. "We need to change our paperwork. We need to change it to say that we are open to a baby girl *or* a baby boy. And we need to add that we are open to special needs."

Throughout my weekend of prayer and crying in the closet, I realized that we had put restrictions on God. We had said yes to adoption but on our own terms. We had told Him yes, but only if it was a healthy baby girl. If we fully trusted God to lead us to our child, then why in the world would we ever put God in a box? I realized as I was distraught at the thought of this sick baby boy who needed a family that it didn't matter to me whether God blessed our family with a girl or a boy, healthy or sick. It was not my place to give God conditions. Again, I needed to let go. I needed to trust God. I needed to hold this with an open hand, not a clenched fist.

There was no possible way for me to fully understand just how much that one phone call would change our lives. On January 5, 2015, seven months after we changed our file, we received *the call*. We had been matched with a birthmother in Ohio. Her name was Grace, and she was just over five months pregnant. She didn't know if she was having a boy or a girl.

If we had not opened up our file to adopting a baby girl *or* a baby boy, then our profile book would never have even made it into this birth mother's hands.

Let God.

One month after being matched, Brian and I sat hand in hand as our plane left the small airport in Eugene and headed for Ohio. We were flying out to spend the weekend with the birthmother of our child—whoa.

After a full day of flying and a three-hour time change, we were grateful to finally pick up our small rental car and find our hotel. We would be meeting Grace the next day, and I definitely needed some sleep and deep-breathing exercises before then.

The sleep never came.

The next morning, we choked down some breakfast and then headed to pick up Grace from her apartment downtown. The drive was quiet.

When we finally arrived and knocked on the door, it was a heartbeat before she answered. It is still a difficult moment to explain. This person was a stranger and yet also one of the most important people in the world to us. She was strong and brave and young. In that moment, I was hit with just how overwhelming this situation actually was. Adoption is an experience of great joy that rises from such great loss. I was going to be this child's mother, the one with the privilege of raising and loving this child, watching first steps and hearing first words, but the woman I was now standing across from was doing something I was not meant to do—she was giving my child life.

We spent the next two days shopping for maternity clothes, going out to lunch, meeting her friends and soaking up every word she was willing to share with us. In the end, we thanked her and hugged her and promised to see her again soon. We were all anxious for the next two months to quickly pass.

And then we headed back to Oregon to wait.

The due date was April 19, and the only important event we had on our calendar for all of 2015 was my youngest sister's wedding on April 17. We like to keep life exciting—and stressful.

I was maid of honor (I refused to be called a *matron*), Davis was ring bearer, and Rory was flower girl. The plan was to be on standby for baby but still plan to be at the wedding. If Grace didn't go into labor before the due date, then we would leave right after the wedding. A lot of moving pieces of a huge, anxiety-filled puzzle.

April 17 arrived and still no phone call. We officially made it to wedding day. We all got dressed up in our fancy clothes and headed over to the stunning outdoor venue. It was a sunny spring day in the Oregon valley—a rare and miraculous occurrence. Rory looked like a tiny fairy princess topped with a crown of flowers, Davis was dressed in his miniature Marine Corps dress blues, complete with plastic sword, and I was just doing my best not to let my nerves make me sweat my makeup off. The ceremony was beautiful and emotional and ran without a hitch—always a worry for a mother with kids in a wedding ceremony. We made our exit down the petal-strewn aisle, enjoyed a feast of a dinner, and then it came time for the toasts. I stood up and spoke words from my heart. I hugged my little sister, and then Brian and I rounded up our crew and headed for the car.

We were going to Ohio.

When I say we were going to Ohio, I mean we were headed to Ohio hillbilly style. We had the SUV loaded down with suitcases, snacks, and a huge stack of DVDs. We changed out of our wedding clothes and put on pajamas, buckled both kids into their car seats, popped in the first Disney movie, and hit the highway.

The plan was to take turns driving and sleeping, and drive straight through to Ohio—and that is exactly what we did. We stopped for gas, meals, and bathroom breaks. We also made the deal with the kids that they could get a gas station souvenir in each state that we traveled through—nothing screams "winning" like a kid with a $4.99 Wyoming gas station shot glass. When it got late, we flipped off the DVD player and told the kids it was bedtime. They contentedly slept through both nights snuggled in their car seats. I'm still not sure how it all worked. It truly had to have been divine intervention.

We drove for forty-three hours straight. We left Oregon on the night of the seventeenth and arrived in Ohio on the evening of the nineteenth. We were exhausted and ready to be out of the car, but the bottom line was that we made it before baby was born. We made it.

We had promised Grace that we would take her out to dinner on the evening we arrived, so after checking into our hotel and changing our clothes, we headed downtown to pick her up. The kids were excited to meet her and she them. She chose a local Golden Corral buffet restaurant where we sat and made small talk until everyone was through with their meals. As we headed for the door, the first strong contraction hit.

It was time.

She struggled to make it back to the car, and we quickly decided that Brian would take Grace and me to the hospital while he and the kids went back to the hotel to wait.

We arrived at the hospital emergency entrance about ten minutes later—though the ride felt long. I mentioned the word *labor* to the check-in staff, and the next thing I knew the nursing staff placed Grace in a wheelchair and checked her into a small room to be evaluated before making any decisions. She was promptly hooked up to fetal monitors, and as soon as the nurse turned on the monitor volume, I was flooded with emotion—I was now hearing the beautiful music of my baby's heartbeat, what an incredible gift as an adoptive mother. As I came out of my daze, I realized that while baby's heartbeat was strong and steady on the monitor, the contractions were not. In fact, it was pretty clear that Grace was *not* in active labor. Now what?

Now that the situation had lost the sense of urgency, the nurse informed us that the doctor would come by shortly and talk about what comes next. So Grace and I waited. And waited. And waited. I was exhausted. I wanted a shower and a bed. Grace was impatient and wanted out of the hospital. We weren't exactly a dream team at this point.

After what felt like hours, a doctor gave the courtesy double knock and then entered the room.

"Well, Grace, you are not in labor." Even though I already knew this fact, the disappointment was strong.

"*But*," the doctor continued, "I talked to the labor-and-delivery team, and they have a room available. Since today is your due date and you are already here and ready to go, we're willing to just induce labor tonight."

I stepped out and called Brian to let him know the new plan. Since Grace was not in active labor, I told him it would still be a while and to go to bed and get some much needed (and earned) rest.

After the arrangements were made, we were moved out of the emergency wing and up to the labor-and-delivery floor. She was given an IV of Pitocin and an epidural and placed on a clear liquid diet to prep for labor. After that, Grace spent the remainder of the night in varying states of agitation, and I did my best to apologize to the nurses and doctors by only using my eyes. Once Grace finally fell asleep, I wandered out into the hall to the vending machine and bought a healthy meal of pink Pop-Tarts and orange juice.

The night passed, and we were still waiting. Progress was slow. The plan was for me to remain with Grace until it was time to push, and then I would leave to give her some privacy. No one else was there. No one came to visit. As I was sitting in the delivery room with a young girl I hardly knew, I realized how difficult and painful this situation really was. Adoption stems from such brokenness, and I was feeling the weight of that. My heart hurt for Grace.

Around 3:30 in the afternoon, things changed. Grace was feeling the pressure, and it was finally time to start pushing. I paged the nurse, and she began the preparation process. As she busied around the room preparing, she coached Grace through contractions. I hovered on the side unsure of my place in the situation. Finally, I came to the conclusion that it was time for me to leave the room and let Grace have her privacy.

I gathered my few things and went to the bedside. "Okay, Grace, I'm going to step out now and sit in the waiting room until you are ready for me to come back. You are doing great. I'm so proud of you."

She didn't even open her eyes. "You can just stay if you want. I don't care."

The nurse and I made eye contact for a brief second, and she gave me a small encouraging smile.

"Oh, okay, sure. I'm happy to stay and be here with you if you would like that."

"Yeah, I'm good with that. Just stay, please."

And so just like that, I was invited to witness the birth of our child. I was also given the invitation to be Grace's person. As I stood beside her hospital bed, I was hit with the reality that we were not just adopting this baby into our family but also welcoming in Grace. This baby would need me soon, but Grace needed me *now*.

At 4:07 p.m., our sweet baby girl entered the world.

The delivery went well, and Grace and baby were both checked off as strong and healthy. The only shock was that the baby was a girl. Grace had been absolutely convinced it was a boy—surprise! I stayed by Grace's side as the nurse explained that she would be taking baby to the nursery to clean her up and take her measurements. Then Grace turned to me and asked, "What are you going to name her?"

"Well, Brian and I discussed that if the baby was a girl we would like to name her Esme. It means 'loved,' and we feel like that is the right fit for her. We would call her May for short. Is that okay with you?"

She nodded her head. "I love it."

Then she looked me straight in the eyes and spoke in a voice that meant business. "You know what I want right now? A bacon cheeseburger." And she smiled.

I laughed and stood up to leave. "I can definitely make that happen."

Grace had seventy-two hours to wait before she could sign the paperwork for the adoption. Every state is different, but in Ohio in was a full, excruciating seventy-two hours.

In the interest of protecting Grace, I'm not going to share all the details of this stage in the process. I also want to protect my daughter's story because truly it is *her* story to share when and if she is ever ready. It is not mine to share. I will say this, though—those seventy-two hours were some of the most heart-wrenching hours in my entire life, but after enduring it, I have more respect for Grace than I ever dreamed possible. She made a difficult and selfless decision in the face of extreme pressure from the world. Birth mothers are some of the most fiercely brave women out there, and that is exactly what I will tell Esme when she is old enough to understand.

After the seventy-two hours were up and the paperwork had been signed, I was able to take a real breath again. Esme was now our daughter. Little Baby May who we had waited and prayed for was finally ours—she was finally home.

At this point in our adoption journey, "home" referred to the hotel where we'd set up camp for the two weeks we were required to remain in the state of Ohio. The two-week mandatory stay was for paperwork to be processed and filed. It was also like boot camp for life with three kids—living in a hotel room with a five-year-old, three-year-old, and newborn was a circus but without the coordinated teamwork. Davis thought it was especially cool to lounge around in his tiny boxer briefs and drink his milk out of the "fancy cups" (aka "wine glasses") from the hotel kitchenette. Rory spent most of her free time being a mermaid in the bathtub (including goggles and ruffled swimsuit) and splashing an ungodly amount of water onto the bath mat. We also purposely booked a hotel with an indoor pool, so several hours of every day were devoted to swimming and expending some energy. Preschooler energy is basically a super power.

We were about a week and a half into our forced vacation and feeling a bit run- down when a miracle happened.

I was down at the complimentary continental hotel breakfast with Esme, attempting to let the rest of the crew sleep past 6:00 a.m. when Jack Hanna and his team came into the breakfast lounge. For those of you who didn't have the privilege of watching his show as kids in the early '90s, Jack Hanna had a morning television program all about animals. I loved his show growing up, and the reruns were now a favorite of my kids as well. And at that very moment, he was eating his breakfast at the table next to me. I repeated to myself to play it cool and not make a fool of myself, and then I quickly shuffled out of the room to go wake the kids!

Brian, Davis, and Rory were not as enthusiastic about running down to breakfast before 7:00 a.m., and I believe now that they thought I had officially lost my mind as I frantically dressed the kids and excitedly rambled on about "Jungle Jack." Finally, when they understood what was actually happening, they picked up their pace, and we all hustled back down to the lounge.

We were totally "those people"—we interrupted his breakfast and sheepishly asked for an autograph. Not only did Jack Hanna stop eating and give our kids his full attention, he had his team get headshot pictures to individually address and sign, he took pictures with the kids, and then he brought out a baby kangaroo in a purse for the kids to hold—seriously, a baby kangaroo in a purse! How cool is this guy!

After we got over being starstruck we settled down and went back to the routine of our hotel breakfast. It was midweek in a small city in Ohio, so the hotel was empty—it was just us, Jack Hanna, his team and the kangaroo at breakfast. He was a down-to-earth guy, and he struck up a conversation with Brian as we all ate in the small lounge. As he and his team got up to leave, he turned back and said, "We are checking out in an hour, and we will be bringing all of the animals back through the lobby if you want to come and meet them?"

Um, yes!

An hour later, we were gathered in the lobby as a parade of

animals were walked right through the hotel lobby and loaded into their tour bus outside the front doors. A penguin waddled past, and to our kids' delight, he pooped on the lobby floor—they still talk about that. Several small critters in cages were carried through. And then the elevator doors opened, and a cheetah and her handler stepped out—I can't imagine the thoughts of a person in an elevator with a cheetah in those last seconds as the doors are closing. To this day, we still have to coach our kids to say that Esme was their favorite part about our trip to Ohio *not* the cheetah.

After our day with Jack Hanna and the animals, we only had one more important thing to complete before we could leave—we had to take Esme in to the doctor for her first checkup. We arrived at the inner-city clinic and quickly met with the young doctor. She said Esme looked perfectly healthy and on track.

As we wrapped up the appointment, she directed her attention from Esme to me and said, "This is your third kiddo, so you are more of a pro than I am. I'm sure you don't have any questions, but just call if you think of something."

"Actually"—I paused unsure of how to phrase my question—"it's true that Esme is my third, but this is actually my first time dealing with a real belly button, and frankly, it is kind of freaking me out. What in the world am I supposed to do with the umbilical cord?" Turns out you do nothing, but I still think it's gross.

Finally, after two weeks of wandering through the limited sites of Ohio, we received clearance to go home. Once the car was loaded to its capacity with suitcases, souvenirs, and children, we hit the road. We were more than ready to go home. The journey home went exactly as you would expect with two tired adults, two preschoolers, and a newborn. Brian quietly drove the car, I was just plain grumpy, Esme ate and pooped every few minutes, and the kids watched *Kung Fu Panda* on repeat for three days straight. But we made it.

The first week of May, exactly three years after we'd started our adoption journey, we arrived back in Oregon as a family of five.

This was not the journey we thought we'd signed up for.

In the adoption community, the verse 1 Samuel 1:27 (NIV) is frequently used. The words are spoken by a woman named Hannah. She has struggled for years to have a child and is now speaking about her beloved son Samuel, she says, "I prayed for this child, and the Lord has granted me what I asked of him." Many cling to this verse like a lifeline through their journey—God will give me what I want!

But what most people miss is in the few verses before it describes Hannah in her wait for Samuel. The verse 1 Samuel 1:16 (NIV) explains that Hannah is praying in "great anguish and grief." The wait was painful. The chapter continues, and Samuel 1:20 (NIV) says, "So in the course of time, Hannah became pregnant and gave birth to a son." Did you catch that? *In the course of time.* It was not immediate, it was not in Hannah's time frame, and it was *hard*. But God had a plan—God had Samuel for Hannah, but she had to have faith and wait on the Lord.

Proverbs 19:21 (NIV) says, "Many are the plans in a person's heart, but it is the Lord's purpose that prevails." And thank goodness for that! I would have completely messed this up. The moment Esme was born, I knew why God had given our journey roadblocks and speed bumps and detours—I knew why He made us wait. It was all to lead us to our daughter—exactly her. It was all a part of His beautiful plan. The true test was if we had enough faith to not give up on the journey when we felt lost. Sometimes life gives us unexpected delays or takes us on a scenic route that we didn't intend to take or even bad directions from a well-meaning friend. Just don't turn back if God has called you to keep going.

God has the map.

He won't let you remain lost.

Just don't turn back.

6 STEPPING OUT OF THE BOAT

Life with three kids meant that we were now officially outnumbered, and we were constantly running on a level of controlled chaos—at least that was what we strived for and even some days that seemed like an unrealistic expectation.

In the fall of 2015, Davis started half-day kindergarten, Rory began preschool a few hours a week, and Esme happily ran the house while they were gone. It was also during this time that we were notified by the Ethiopia adoption program that due to the program closing we had a small window of time to transfer a portion of our fees to another program or they would permanently be forfeited and our contract terminated.

I sat on the small beige love seat in the living room staring into the fire that was silently bringing comfort and warmth to the house. I looked up at Brian, who sat on the couch opposite me and soberly said, "I don't think this feels right. I think we are meant to stop here." I had tears in my eyes and the words seemed to physically hurt. I was saying no to a child in need. Brian just quietly nodded. I knew he agreed, but the words were difficult to say.

"The thing is"—I paused, searching my mind for the right words—"I still have this strong feeling in my gut that God has another child for us but not through this program and not right now." And I meant it.

With that difficult conversation, we walked away from our first adoption process. The program officially closed, all of our fees were forfeited, and our contract was terminated. Sometimes saying no to one thing just means waiting for the right thing to say yes to—but man, it's hard.

Time passed and life went on. Davis broke his arm on the kindergarten playground, showing off for the girls; Rory gained adorable glasses and freckles; and Esme discovered the joy of freestyle toddler dancing in the living room and developed a pretty intense crush on Bruno Mars in the process. We also added a miniature Australian shepherd puppy named Rhett to the family. He really isn't essential to this story, but I just love him so much I felt like I needed to include him—people who overly love their dogs will understand.

In the winter of 2016, Brian came home with the news that he had received the transfer for which we had hoped and prayed for years. We were moving out of the rainy Willamette Valley to sunny, high-desert Central Oregon.

Change is always tough, but God was clearly at work in this move. Our house had a full-price offer before it was even live on the market, we were scheduled to close on the house one week before Brian's new position start date, and we miraculously found a rental home in Redmond that met all of our needs, including amazing landlords. But then we started the packing portion of our move. Moving is never enjoyable or easy, but moving with kids and a puppy is pure torture. I would put things in a box, turn around to get more items, and Esme would promptly unload everything I had just packed. It was a slow and painful process. Eventually, we somehow managed to pack up every last item we had built our life with in Albany.

As we added the last few items to the moving truck, I realized that although I was excited for the next adventure God had for us, it was still emotional to close this chapter. This was the house Brian and I had built our family in, the house we'd brought our children home from the hospital to, the house our children had learned to walk in and the stairs they'd learned to climb and occasionally fall down. This was the only home our children had ever known. But as I walked through the now empty house, it hit me that everything that really mattered was coming with us. I closed the red front door, the one I had painted myself, and jumped in the truck and smiled the whole way over the mountains to our new home in Central Oregon.

We quickly settled into our new life and never looked back. It was clear that this was exactly where God wanted us.

As spring rolled around and the snow melted away, Brian and I made the brave decision to leave the kids with my parents and escape to Hawaii to celebrate our ten-year anniversary. We had not been good about making time for just us, and this seemed like the perfect excuse to do that. Marriage is not easy, but nothing worth the work ever is. We decided to celebrate our decade together by renewing our wedding vows on the beach, and we spent the week relaxing and remembering why we chose each other over ten years ago. Little did we know that God was giving us this week to rest and refuel for what was to come.

In April of 2017, Brian and I again sat in our living room on the exact same furniture as before, only in a different home this time, and struggled to work through what God had put on our hearts.

We were being called to adopt again.

We agreed to pray and wait on God to lead us to the right adoption program, which ultimately meant the right child, the child He had created for our family.

Over the next two months, we waited and prayed. We knew a lot more about adoption this time around, and we were already familiar with most programs and requirements, and yet nothing felt quite right. We just couldn't commit. It wasn't until late May that we decided to look at the Rainbow Kids website. The website states that its purpose is "Adoption and Child Welfare Advocacy," and the main reason prospective families visit this site is that it holds a waiting-child list. This is literally a list of thousands of waiting children. The website explains the term "waiting children" like this:

> Generally speaking, all children who are waiting for a family are waiting children. So, it doesn't really matter what category children fall into—they all need forever families. More technically speaking, waiting children have been declared orphans by their country's governing agencies, and their paperwork has been prepared for adoption. However, the term "waiting children" can take on a variety of contexts and meaning depending on the country in which they live. In an attempt to make things simple, a

very basic understanding of waiting children is that they are typically children who are older, have more significant medical special needs, or is a sibling group—all characteristics that often present difficulties in finding families. As a result of the difficulty in finding families, we often have the privileged opportunity of advocating for these precious children. Also, waiting children have often been available for adoption for a longer period than other children.

Waiting children are exactly that—waiting. Waiting for a family. Waiting for love and hope. Waiting to be chosen. As the site explains, these kids have *significant* needs and therefore are difficult to place. So as I opened up this list of almost four thousand profiles of waiting children, I prayed for God to lead us to our child if he or she was listed here.

It was overwhelming scrolling through picture after picture. How would I know if our child was here? How would he or she be different from the other 3,999? And how in the world do you justify saying no to all the others? It was painful, and I could only look at the profiles in short periods of time, but I knew I needed to be doing this. I was actively searching for our child.

And then I saw "Noah." That wasn't his real name, just his file name, but one I will never forget. As I stared at his picture, I began to cry. I knew he was different. He was so tiny and frail. Next to his picture was a list of his special needs—heart defect, thalassemia, and cleft palate. I figured it was pretty good that I knew what two out the three medical conditions were. I also noticed that his birthday was in the fall of 2015—the exact same time we had decided to walk away from our first adoption because we felt God had a different plan for our family. Maybe Noah was the reason.

I walked downstairs in a fog and handed the tablet to Brian with Noah's profile still on the screen. Brian was quiet and stared at the profile for a long time. When he finally looked up, he had tears in his eyes and said words I will always remember, "How could we say no?" That really was the bottom line—How could we say no? What reason could possibly be good enough? He handed back the tablet and I hit the button on his profile to request his file.

On May 31, we received Noah's official file and medical information from the agency he was connected with. The agency instructed us to have a doctor (or several) review the file before we could take the next step. It was important that we understood what we were saying yes to.

As soon as the file arrived in my email, we opened it and did our best to wade through it. Even though the translated file was difficult to understand and piece together, it was clear that Noah had a complicated case. We had been made aware about some of the medical conditions, but new and scary words popped off the screen— "potential brain damage," "potential liver damage," "jaundice," "developmentally delayed." He was sick, but just how sick we needed a medical professional to tell us.

I immediately called several medical offices and requested to have the file reviewed. Though all were willing to review the file, some promised more speed than others. I promptly sent off all the information we had and then carried my cell phone around, impatiently waiting for a return phone call.

A few hours later I got the first call.

"Hello, may I speak to Jordyn Glaser?"

"Speaking," I said a little too eagerly.

"This is Dr. Young and I have reviewed the file you sent over earlier today." There was a pause as he searched for the right place to start. "Noah is very sick, and it is my professional opinion that he should be considered failure to thrive, and we would need to discuss lifelong treatment."

The rest of the conversation continued down this road. We discussed the possibility that Noah would not survive and, if he did, then we would need to consider long-term care. His heart valve was leaking, his diagnosis of thalassemia was a blood disorder that would require regular and frequent blood transfusions, the severe jaundice most likely resulted in the liver and brain damage, the cleft palate would require surgery and intense ongoing therapy, and then we reached the topic of Noah's development. The bottom line was that his development was so behind that he was not even anywhere close to being on the growth chart. He was extremely underweight, and he was just not developing properly physically or mentally.

I did my best to listen and understand the weight of each word. As we wrapped up the conversation, the doctor hesitated and then spoke carefully but with purpose.

"You have other children, I believe? Well, I think you really need to think about the quality of life for your entire family before you move forward with this case."

"Thank you for your time, Dr. Young. I really appreciate your help."

I hung up the phone and turned to Brian, who had been attempting to listen in on the conversation as much as possible.

"We have to hurry." I spoke the words, and then the tears came.

I cried hard. Ugly, gasping for air kind of crying. God was asking us to adopt this little boy. He was asking us to say yes to a sick child, and I could not have felt less qualified for the task. As Brian and I sat on the floor of the bathroom, we boiled it down to the fact that Noah needed a family and his health and development should never determine his worth. This little boy deserved a chance at growing up with a mom and a dad, brothers and sisters. He deserved a chance to feel loved, he deserved medical care and education, and he deserved a chance to know Jesus—and his health should not determine if he was worthy of that.

And as we considered our other children as the doctor suggested, we decided that we could only pray that they would see their parents giving the value of a life and the value of following Christ a higher priority than chasing comfort. As I sat on the bathroom floor, I began to slow my breathing and calm my mind, and it became perfectly clear—we needed to say yes because I was more afraid of missing God's call and God's blessing than I was afraid of doing the hard things. I was not enough for the task at hand, but God was. He had control, and I just needed to keep faithfully following Him and keep saying yes when He asked.

The next day, we submitted our official application to adopt Noah, and with that, we began the hustle of the adoption process all over again. We received preapproval from China two weeks later, and we were given the projected timeline of approximately twelve months to bring Noah home. The caseworker projected that, with our specific case, we would travel to China sometime in April (or later), and she was very clear that the process couldn't move faster than that due to necessary steps between the United States and China. I heard her words and her logic. I understood completely. But I also believed that

God could move mountains, so that week I began *specifically* asking God to bring our son home in January. I was asking for the process to take seven months instead of the normal twelve months. I was asking for a miracle. And I believed He could do it.

Over the next three weeks, we worked hard to quickly gather all the necessary home-study and dossier paperwork—financial information, fingerprints, blood work, background checks, and so on. We were in the race against time. Our little boy needed to get home quickly, and that fact alone was pure motivation. We also took this time to choose a name for our son, and after several family meetings and many chaotic voting sessions, we chose the name Abel.

On the afternoon of July 6, things took an unexpected turn. Shortly after returning home from our regular school pickup routine, my phone chimed, notifying me of a new email. I didn't know just how much our world was about to shift in a matter of moments. I opened the email to the following letter from the agency director:

> Dear Families,
>
> The CCCWA published a notice on their website last night that implemented some changes to the eligibility guidelines for adoptive families. The notice does not specify if it affects families who already have preapproval or a log-in date. WACAP **expects and hopes** that those who are already logged-in or already have preapproval for a specific waiting child will not be impacted; however, we will be contacting the CCCWA to seek clarification on this point and several others.

Some of the guidelines are looser than in the past, whereas some are more restrictive. Below is a summary of the changes as we currently understand them. We have also attached a copy of the notice so that you can review the words exactly as the CCCWA has written them if you wish.

· For married couples, there should be no more than five minor children living in the home. For single parents, there should be no more than two minor children living in the home.

· The youngest child in the home should be at least three years old

· If a parent has a history of skin, thyroid, breast, or testicular cancer, it should be "cured" for at least three years. For other kinds of cancer, it should be "cured" for at least five years.

· There is no longer an income or net-worth exception for those living in a low-cost area (except for families living in China).

· If a married couple has no divorces or one divorce, then the marriage length requirement is two years.

· Married couples with two divorces are still required to be married at least five years.

· Length of cohabitation before marriage counts toward marriage length.

· There needs to be a one-year interval between the placement of a child and the "current adoption application date" of the next adoption. (We are seeking clarification as to whether the "current adoption application date" means dossier log-in date or if it means preapproval date for a second child. We suspect it means log-in date.)

· Families are no longer allowed to adopt two unrelated children simultaneously

· If a family lives overseas, they can only adopt from China if that country also has a "cooperative relationship with China in intercountry adoption" or is also part of the Hague

If you believe that one of these guidelines impacts your family and you do not have preapproval or a log-in date, please contact your case manager. We will be reaching out to families who we believe may be affected by these guideline changes. If we learn that the changes will affect other families who are further along in the adoption process, we will let you know immediately. Please do not hesitate to contact me with questions or concerns.

I finished reading with tears in my eyes. Esme was not yet three years old. We no longer met China's requirements. We were going to lose Abel.

I spent the next several minutes on the phone to our caseworker, trying to sort out the details. She explained that all the agencies who partner with China were in a scramble to find out how these new guidelines affected families who were already in the process and matched with a child. She promised to call as soon as they got the answers. I hung up the phone and dropped to my knees and prayed.

"Father, please don't take our little boy away. Please."

I continued to talk to God throughout the afternoon and evening while I waited for a phone call with news from the agency. I trusted God's plan, but I didn't pretend to understand it. I questioned why He would ask us to say yes to this adoption, to break our hearts for this sweet boy, and then so swiftly take him away from us.

I didn't understand, but I still trusted.

Our caseworker had explained that the only thing that was going to let us keep moving forward with this adoption was the fact that we already had our "preapproval" from China. It was hard waiting for answers, but in those several hours of waiting and praying, I realized that if we had not acted on God's call *exactly* when we had, when it still felt overwhelming and scary and uncomfortable, we would not have had our preapproval in time to beat these new requirements.

At 8:13 p.m. that same evening, we got the news we had been waiting for. Due to our preapproval status, we were allowed to continue the adoption process. Again, I dropped to my knees, and this time I thanked God—thank you for not taking our little boy. As I prayed my words of gratitude, I was reminded of my gasping ugly tears on the bathroom floor. If I had waited for my own comfort to do what God was asking, we would have missed our chance. We had received our preapproval only two weeks before the new requirements were put in place—our doubt would have lost us our son. We cannot wait for the fear to subside and for the task to have no risk—we just need to have faith and say yes.

As June rolled into July, we continued the hustle to complete our home study as quickly as possible. Every day mattered. On July 9, we were scheduled to complete our home visits and inspections with our assigned home-study caseworker. It was scheduled for several hours on a Sunday afternoon. This was our third home study, so we were much less nervous and anxious. This time around, I didn't bother to reorganize the towel closet and dust the air vents. I didn't even bother to do the dishes after breakfast before we left for church that morning. I had finally learned the home-study process was not about perfection, and I could relax a bit.

After we left church, we stopped to grab sandwiches from the deli before we arrived home so we could have a quick (and minimally messy) lunch before the caseworker arrived. We unloaded from the car and gathered around the table to eat. We had less than an hour before the visit. As we ate our sandwiches and kept reminding our kids to "just focus and eat," Davis looked over my shoulder, creased his brow, and said, "What's *that*?" Since it was July and we not only kept the windows open regularly but the kids frequently ran in and out of the back door to play in the yard, I expected to look behind me and see a fly on the wall—that was not what I saw.

The five of us were silent for a moment as we tried to process the sight before us. There was a huge water bubble under the latex paint that had started from the ceiling and had run down to the middle of the wall. It looked like our wall was upset and now had one massive crocodile tear running down its otherwise perfectly smooth face.

"*What* in the world?" I finally spoke aloud. "Well, now what?" I turned to Brian for a magic solution to our ridiculous problem.

"Um—well—I guess we drain the water and pray for the best." We looked at each other with our eyebrows raised, shook our heads and began to laugh. Welcome to the spiritual battle of adoption. This was the expired smoke detectors all over again!

We quickly found a razor blade and made a small incision at the bottom of the bubble. I had placed towels on the carpet below and stood ready with a towel against the wall to soak up the leak. As I stood at the wall mopping up the water, Brian went in search of the source. Our caseworker would be arriving soon, and we still had no idea what had made our wall cry. It appeared that whatever had caused the leak had stopped for now because the bubble was not refilling, so at least that was a good sign. We did our best to dry the wall and the carpet and then smooth the now very wrinkled paint on the wall. Just as we finished cleaning up, the doorbell rang, and our home-study visit began.

The interviews and inspection went just as planned. The now wrinkled wall wasn't even mentioned. Our home-study process was complete, and now we just had to wait to receive the written report and official approval from our caseworker, which would take another two weeks or so.

(Just to wrap up the mystery for readers—after our visit, we continued the search for the source of the leak and discovered that our showerhead upstairs had a steady drip into the shower. The drip was hitting the faucet handle and then traveling back into the wall resulting in our crying wall—absolutely ridiculous.)

While we waited for our home-study report to be submitted, we also worked on other steps in the process, including sending our US immigration (USCIS) application and payment. As I sat at my desk signing the check to USCIS for $945, an email popped up on my computer screen. We had been running a T-shirt fund-raiser for the last month that had recently ended, and the email was notifying me of our payment for the fund-raiser. I set down my pen and opened the email. Exactly $963 was now being transferred directly into our bank account from the fund-raiser—$18 more than the check I was currently writing.

When people find out that we have adopted, unfortunately, one of the first questions is about the cost. I hate it, but that's just normally the case. In response to this question, I always return with the truth—yes, adoption is expensive, but it is also testimony of how the Lord provides. God has always provided just enough when we needed it. Did we win the lottery? No, but we never missed a payment or didn't have enough. The problem is that you must say yes to God in faith and then watch how He provides, not wait for Him to provide and *then* say yes. That is not faith. That is comfort and reassurance. God calls us to walk out in faith and trust Him enough even if we don't have all the answers. When something is from God, He will give us what we need to accomplish his plan—He even gave us an extra $18 to treat ourselves.

On July 31, our home-study report was officially approved. This was a huge step toward bringing Abel home, and the Devil knew it. The same week we received our home-study approval, our new-to-us Suburban blew a head gasket, I required an insane amount of unexpected dental work (something I had never had in my thirty-two years of life), and—the one that finally brought me to tears—my entire thirty-two-ounce water bottle spilled into my purse and soaked everything including the Bible I had loved and studied for over a decade. The battle was real.

By the end of that week I was confident that we were on the right track. Otherwise, the enemy wouldn't be fighting so hard. When we live a life of comfort, we are not a threat, and the Devil can just leave us alone. After the week we had endured, it was evident we were on the Devil's radar. But rather than becoming weighed down with discouragement and defeat, it seemed to have the opposite effect on me—it fueled and encouraged me to be a threat. I want to fight the good fight, I want to get to heaven out of breath and hear the words "well done," and I'm not going to do that by playing it safe. So as I used my hair dryer to individually dry the pages of my soaked Bible, I put my shoulders back and mumbled, "Bring it," and then I kept going.

Our dossier was sent to China on November 9. The dossier is a packet of all the official and original documents sent to the foreign country you're adopting from. If you talk to any adoptive family about their dossier, you'll notice a degree of passion that arises in their voices. You'll never buy more insurance when sending a package in the mail than you will with this thick envelope filled with your *entire* life.

This milestone started the clock on our process with China. Once the partnership begins, it is on a fairly rigid schedule. There are just too many necessary steps to complete to alter the timeframe. The normal schedule is to receive a log-in date one to two weeks after the dossier was sent to China, receive the letter seeking confirmation two to three months after the log-in date, and then receive travel approval one to two months after the letter seeking confirmation. With our dossier sent the beginning of November and taking into consideration the Christmas and New Years' holidays, we were told to expect to travel to China in mid-to-late April. April was definitely not January. Although I was hit with a wave of discouragement by our projected timeline, I was determined not to lose hope. I continued to ask God for a miracle. I continued to *specifically* ask for January.

The day after our dossier was sent, I left for my annual local adoptive/foster mama weekend retreat. It was something I looked forward to every year. It was a weekend filled with worship, training, rest, and friendship. Fuel for a tired mama's heart.

As I spent the weekend talking, crying, and praying with fellow adoptive mothers, God was already at work orchestrating something bigger than I could have ever imagined. On the second day of the retreat, I bumped into a mom who I had talked to at the retreat in the previous years. We began catching up on life and family, and eventually I was sharing all about our current adoption situation. As I spoke with tears in my eyes about my sense of urgency to bring Abel home and shared the list of medical needs we were about to take on, she gave me a funny look. My words faltered midsentence, and I paused to let her speak.

"I have a friend with a son from China who has thalassemia. It is one of the few medical conditions that China allows a case to be expedited for. I think you can file to expedite Abel's case!"

We stared at each other for a moment, before smiling—I had no words.

That night I went back to my hotel room and wrote out an email to our caseworker. It was short and to the point—we wanted to expedite Abel's case, and we wanted to do it now. I sent off the email and then spent the rest of the weekend praying for God to move mountains.

On Monday morning, our caseworker promptly responded, agreeing to make the request, but she was very clear that it was up to the officials in China and the orphanage whether the case would be expedited. She was making no promises. She explained how this new process would play out and asked that we obtain letters from the doctors who had reviewed Abel's medical file expressing the urgency needed in this case. Then I reached the bottom of the email, and my breath caught in my chest.

> We roughly estimate you'll travel as early as January
> if all goes smoothly.

I reread the last line—January. If all goes well, we would travel in January. As I sat there soaking in the latest development, I was blown away by God's hand in this journey. God was on the move, and we had been given a front-row seat to watch Him work.

On November 14, we received our dossier log-in date from China only five days after being sent. Six days later, we received our letter seeking confirmation. And another four weeks after that, we received our official travel approval. A process that was meant to take five-and-a-half months took five-and-a-half weeks.

As Christmas rapidly approached, my heart ached to have Abel home. I hung a stocking for him alongside the rest of the family's and held on to the fact that this was his last Christmas in an institution and without a family. God being the good father that He is provided exactly the soothing balm my heart needed—on December 22, we received an update from the orphanage, including photos and a video. I smiled at the computer screen as I watched my sweet boy in the short video clip. I watched it again and again, wiping tears from my eyes as I hit replay.

That same day, we got a call from the agency to let us know we had officially been given our appointment with the Chinese consulate, and we could now book our flights to China. Our appointment date was set for January 17, which meant we would be taking custody of Abel the week prior on January 8.

God did it: we were leaving for China the first week of January.

God is fully capable of moving mountains, but He needs us to say yes when the call is still scary. He needs us to leave our desire for comfort and control behind. He needs us to get out of the boat and trust Him.

7 SURRENDERING

On January 6, 2018, we flew out of our small-town airport in Oregon with the final destination of Guangzhou, China. Our first connection was only a few short hours away in San Francisco, California. The small plane landed, and we headed to the nearest deli for coffee and breakfast. As we relaxed at our small table waiting for our food, I watched the hustle and bustle in the trendy restaurant. The small space was packed with rushing people and buzzing with constant noise. But as I stared around the crowd, a familiar face caught my eye—there on the TV screen next to the coffee bar was none other than Jack Hanna. We decided it was a lucky sign, and we had a pretty good laugh as our breakfast arrived.

A few hours later, we were boarding our next connecting flight. As I walked down one of the two aisles in the airplane, I knew that the plane's size was in direct correlation to just how insanely long this next flight would be. We found our seats and got comfortable—we were going to be here a while.

Finally, after twenty-plus hours in the air and a brutal time change, we finally arrived in Guangzhou late on the night of January 7. We collected our bags, found our guide, and boarded the shuttle to our hotel. The guide was welcoming but direct. Being an adoption guide was her job, and therefore, she was professional and to the point. As for us, this situation was anything but business; it was *all* personal. We arrived at the hotel exhausted from traveling yet completely confused as to if it was day or night. We did our best to sleep. We knew the importance of getting some good rest because the next day we would be taking custody of our son. It was our last night as a family of five.

When the clock, not our bodies, told us it was the appropriate time to get up in the morning, we did our best to function. Jet lag at that level is no joke. We found our way down to the hotel breakfast buffet and then met several other American families in the lobby as we waited for the van to take us to the civil-affairs office. Everyone was anxious, and the nerves were starting to really set in. It was game time.

We loaded into the shuttle van and took the quiet ride to the civil-affairs building. I tried to keep track of the roads we were taking as we raced through the crowded streets of Guangzhou, but soon it was too much to process for my overly full brain—I switched over my efforts to deep breathing instead.

We pulled into a dingy alleyway lined with dumpsters and found the unmarked entrance to a tall building. Our guide held the door as we filed into the dim lobby that contained two elevator doors and not much more. We took the elevators up, and the doors opened to a brightly lit room filled with families huddled in small groups around the room—all waiting for their children. I looked over at Brian and raised my eyebrows. This was it.

We stepped out of the elevators and headed to an open couch close to the window. Our guide brought us paperwork to sign and told us to just wait where we were while she checked in. I glanced around the large room to see approximately eight or so other families quietly doing the exact same thing we were. There was a low murmur of voices, but mainly the room was just filled with nerves. Our guide shuffled back over to our corner of the room and told us that Abel and his caregivers had been delayed in traffic and were currently not in the building as had been planned. We were going to have to sit and wait a bit longer. I nodded that I understood and tried to keep breathing. No one needed a crazy blond American having a panic attack.

As we waited for Abel to arrive, the officials began to gather families one by one to the center of the room. As a family stood at the focal point of the room, an office door directly across from them would open, and a caregiver carrying a child would enter. The caregiver would walk quietly to the family and hand over the now screaming child. The new mother or father would hold the child tightly and do everything in their power to soothe the terrified child while the guides and officials took pictures and video of the overwhelming scene. After a few minutes of this, the next family would be called up to the center of the room, and the bizarre scenario would repeat itself all over again.

All the while, we waited for our turn. Waited for Abel.

After about forty-five minutes of waiting and watching all the families be united with their children, two women entered the room in a rush, and one of them was carrying a small child on her back. We couldn't see the child's face because he was bundled in a large winter coat and hat, but we knew it was him. That was the first glimpse I had of our son.

They walked directly to the office where the caregivers and children had been gathered and closed the door behind them. More waiting.

Finally, our guide came out of the office and called us to the center of the room—it was our turn. We were the last family. Brian, Davis, and I awkwardly stood together, staring intently at the office door waiting for it to open. And when it finally did, I held my breath. There was Abel, so tiny and completely calm. The caregiver handed him over to me, and he didn't cry like the other children, but his silence scared me even more. We stood and let the guides finish taking pictures and videos of the moment. I knew down the road I would want those pictures, but in that moment, I just wanted to bolt.

We returned to our corner and sat on the couch with Abel. The caregivers and our guide followed us over and pulled up chairs to sit across from us. We had a few minutes to ask questions about Abel before we would all part ways.

I handed Abel to Brian and pulled out a small notebook that I had written down questions to remember to ask just in case my brain was too overwhelmed to function on the spot. I definitely was grateful for the notebook. We took turns asking our guide questions in English, the guide translating, the caregivers responding in Mandarin, and then the translation again. It was a complicated dance.

"What does he eat? And how often does he eat?"

"Rice cereal from a bottle or rice porridge about five times a day starting at 5:00 a.m. Just prop him up to eat."

Then she handed us a baby bottle with a large hole popped

through the nipple so the rice cereal would be able to get through. I tried to keep my hand from shaking as I took the bottle.

"Has he ever taken a bath?"

"He has been washed down in a small basin."

"Does he walk yet?"

"No."

"Does he have any words in Mandarin?"

"No."

"How can I soothe him when he gets upset?"

"He doesn't really get upset, but if he does then do this—"

She reached out and roughly patted his cheek three times and then looked back at me as if this had clearly answered my question. Then she turned to our guide and rapidly spoke in Mandarin, obviously saying something of importance, as our guide raised her eyebrows while listening before turning to us with the translation.

"She said that the child was just discharged from the hospital two days ago after being treated for pneumonia, so it is important that you keep him warm, especially if going outside."

My mind tried to process this. This small child now sitting on my lap was mine and yet so far from feeling that way. He had recently been admitted to the hospital for a week, and I have to hear about it as an afterthought from the caregiver. The thought of him being alone in a hospital bed hurt my heart. I nodded my head indicating that we understood and would be diligent about keeping him warm.

And then our time was up. We made arrangements to visit the orphanage later in the week, thanked them for caring for our son the first two years of his life and then gathered our things and exited the building with Abel. That was it.

We loaded back into our shuttle van and returned to the hotel conference room to sign documents with our guide. She explained that we would be returning to the same civil-affairs office building the next day to officially complete the adoption.

"I thought that was what we just did today?" I said feeling very confused. We left the building with our child, that felt pretty complete to me.

"No, you return tomorrow for the official interview and documents. You can still change your mind." She said this very matter-of-factly, but her words made my stomach turn. "It happens," she added when she saw the horrified look on our faces. I didn't push the conversation any further because my heart and brain were already overwhelmed by the emotions of today.

After preparing all the documents for the next day, we decided that we would return to our room for a short rest and hopefully a bath and change of clothes for Abel before dinner. Once in the room, we figured the best way to start was to feed Abel a bottle and then gradually start to remove all the oversized layers of clothes before getting him into the bath.

We fumbled through making the bottle. How warm should we make the water? How much rice cereal should we mix in? All the instructions on the box of rice cereal were in Mandarin (obviously), and we knew nothing about this little boy who was now supposed to be ours. I cried as I inadequately mixed the bottle—I had no idea how to be this child's mama.

Before giving him his bottle, we removed his large parka. It was white with fake-fur lining the hood and rhinestones across the front. It was also a child's size 6—not baby or toddler size. His small hand reached to about the place the elbow should be. Instantly, he seemed half the size. I scooped him up and handed him the bottle. His response was frantic. He grabbed the bottle with his tiny hands and gulped as fast as he possibly could manage. I looked at Brian, my mouth open and eyebrows raised. "Should I take it from him so he can come up for air?" By the time I looked back down at the small body in my arms, he had finished the bottle. He was now lying in my arms catching his breath.

Over the next hour, we removed more layers of clothing from his frail frame—another overly large, blue quilted jacket and matching pant set, tiny socks, bright-red shoes with a Peppa Pig design, and a white onesie—until finally he was down to his diaper and ready to take a bath. I held back tears as we looked him over. His bony kneecaps were wider than his thighs. His head was completely bald on the sides and back because he rarely was up off the floor. The skin on his forehead was scaly and peeling because when he crawled his neck wasn't strong enough to keep his head up, so he dragged his head along the floor. Brian and I looked at each other but had no words.

We put about an inch of lukewarm water in the bathtub, had the soap and shampoo ready to go, and even added a small rubber duck to the water to hopefully be a happy distraction. Then we put Abel in. Brian held onto Abel's torso for necessary support, and Abel tightly clung to the edge of the tub. He was intrigued by the water and didn't seem afraid, but he also had no intention of sitting down in the water. We did our best to introduce him gently and patiently to this new experience; we didn't want this to be traumatizing for him. Brian showed him how to splash the water while I attempted to use a washcloth to clean him off. After a few minutes, we felt satisfied that while he might not be perfectly clean, he was definitely a lot less grimy, and the bottom line was that we didn't want to push him too far with too many new experiences in one day.

After bath and dinner, we all sat in the hotel room attempting to relax and let the dust settle from our first day together. We were exhausted from the day and the jet lag, so when it finally reached an appropriate bedtime for Abel, we all decided to go to bed. We laid Abel in the crib, and once again he didn't cry—he had yet to cry all day, a fact that was beginning to terrify me. I attempted to rub his head (because that's what mamas do to their babies at bedtime), but it quickly became clear that my touch was not soothing to him. I gently placed the blanket over his tiny body and whispered, "I love you, buddy," a phrase that had no meaning to him yet but something I was determined to show him.

I climbed into the twin bed next to Davis and silently cried myself to sleep.

A few hours after falling asleep, I woke up and didn't know why at first. There was a strange sound but in my foggy state I had no idea what it was or where it was coming from. I got out of bed and shuffled the few steps over to Abel's crib. He was not crying; he was rocking. He was on his hands and knees rocking back and forth. My eyes welled up with tears as I scooped him up and held him close. I considered not sharing the gritty details because they hurt, and frankly they are just not what people want to hear, but I'm sharing because they are also very real. I'm sharing because millions of children around the world cry at night with nobody coming. I'm sharing because I have now seen firsthand the effects of what happens to a child when they feel unloved.

Hold your babies tight. If you have them, hold them. At night when they cry out for you, hold them close. Rub their backs and stroke their hair. Let them feel safe and loved. Even on the tough days after the millionth toddler tantrum about the wrong color sippy cup or how you cut their sandwich into squares instead of triangles—hold them. They need you.

It was a rough night, and when 3:30 a.m. finally rolled around, Davis and I were both the victims of unrelenting jet lag, and we were up for the day. Luckily, all the rooms in our hotel were designed with the bedroom and bathroom separated from the living space with a sliding pocket door. We quietly wandered into the living room to have a snack and zone out watching Chinese TV shows.

About five hours later, Abel and Brian woke up, and we got ready for our big day back at the civil-affairs office. Today, we would make the adoption paperwork official. Abel guzzled down another bottle, and then we headed downstairs to the hotel continental breakfast before catching our shuttle. Even though we had no idea where to begin with food ideas for Abel, we picked a few soft items for him to try like scrambled eggs and tofu—he turned nothing away.

After breakfast, we met in the lobby with the other families, all of whom looked like they had just survived some type of natural disaster. Everyone appeared a bit dazed and disheveled—but the head count was correct, meaning everyone had survived through the first night.

We boarded the car-seat-free and seatbelt-free van—not ideal for toddlers, especially ones who had rarely if ever been in a car before. We endured the wild ride back to the civil-affairs building, and as we rode the elevator up to the office, we put our game faces on. Today, we entered with a sense of purpose—today, we would flat-out lie and tell every official in the building that we were confident in our abilities to parent this sweet little boy.

My hands were shaky throughout the interview, and I focused on nodding and smiling a lot. The caseworker read off the list of

Abel's special needs and required our verbal confirmation that we understood exactly what we were taking on. Again, we held firm in our belief that his needs had zero connection with his worth. When we reached the end of our interview, she asked one last question,

"Are you satisfied with this child?"

My stomach turned at the brokenness and the coldness of this question. This was an official interview question, and she stared at us as she waited for our verbal answer. I sat up a little straighter in my chair as Brian and I both said with confidence and some degree of defiance, "Absolutely." She nodded her head and signed and stamped the documents. Abel was now officially our son.

Once all of our documents had been stamped, signed, and sealed, we left the civil-affairs office and headed for the shopping center. Our next major priority was finding clothes that somewhat fit Abel's tiny figure. Before we left for China, I had gathered baby clothing in various sizes and styles because I wasn't exactly sure what he would need. He was two and a half years old, but I knew he was very small for his age, so I assumed taking twelve-month clothing and eighteen-month clothing *should* work fairly well. I assumed wrong. He was absolutely swimming in the clothing I brought, and we literally couldn't keep his pants from sliding off his nonexistent waist. The reality was that Abel weighed under twenty pounds and was closer to the size of a nine-month-old. We walked through the mall, entertained by the shops and styles, until we found a children's clothing store that seemed to be the closest to our taste. I weaved through the store straight to the sales rack in the back and grabbed several pairs of pants in size six-to-nine months, all with one very crucial feature—they all had a functional drawstring to cinch down the waist as far as possible.

Over the next three days, we were able to mix necessary

appointments (like applying for Abel's passport) with a bit of local sightseeing. It was quickly apparent to us that Abel could only handle short outings; otherwise, he would start to become overwhelmed and display self-harm behaviors. The guide explained to us that Abel had probably never been outside before, let alone to the market or a museum. We knew we needed to go at Abel's pace and do our best to remember that literally *everything* was new to him—even the people he was with.

January 13 was our eleventh wedding anniversary (cheers to eleven years of not killing each other). It was also the day of Abel's mandatory medical appointment at the government hospital. This appointment was a crucial step to receiving clearance for Abel to leave China. As we entered the hospital, I was immediately stunned by the mass of people milling around. Babies were crying, mothers were pacing, and impatient older children were running throughout the room. It was pure chaos and anxiety. I was handed a clipboard and told that we would have four exams in four separate rooms—general checkup, hearing screen, measurements, and a blood draw to test for tuberculosis.

On one side of the massive room were four doors that families were regularly entering and exiting all appearing highly stressed and praying that this circus would soon be over. I completed our paperwork, and we got in line with the other families. When it was finally our turn, we were called up to door number 1, the general exam. The nurses took height, weight, and vitals and then a doctor brought in Abel's medical file. He skeptically asked us if we fully understood all of the medical needs Abel had been diagnosed with, and after we confirmed that we did, he sent us to door number 2.

In the second exam room, we sat through a sad excuse of a hearing screen. The doctor then looked in Abel's ears, nose, and mouth. He asked us if we knew about Abel's cleft palate and if we planned to have it fixed. Oh, you mean the gaping hole in his mouth? Yes, we knew. And yes we intended to have it repaired. On to door number 3.

They took all of Abel's measurements, one more box checked off. And then we came to door number 4.

At this door, the atmosphere felt different. The parents here looked worried, and one mother was pacing nervously next to the door. It became clear why when the door opened and a masked nurse handed over a screaming toddler to the pacing mother and then routinely called the next name. The parents were not allowed to go in with their child for the blood draw. We had just spent the last five days doing everything in our power to bond and build trust with Abel, and now we had to hand him over to someone who would hurt and terrify him. I pulled him in a little tighter as we listened to the screams from behind the door and waited for our turn. What a nightmare.

After completing the entire ordeal, we boarded our shuttle bus with all the other exhausted families from our group. As we drove back to the hotel, the guide explained that we were now done with all the medical appointments unless by some chance our child's TB test came back positive.

"A positive TB test is very rare. The odds are less than 1 percent. But I am required to tell you this just in case. If by chance your child tests positive, then I will bring you and your child back to the hospital for more testing. In all my years as an adoption guide, I have only had one case when a child tested positive for TB, so don't worry."

And at the conclusion of her precautionary speech, we arrived at the hotel and wearily headed up to our room. We decided that for our next anniversary we would go somewhere more relaxing.

The next day, I was scheduled to visit the orphanage. The drive was twelve hours round trip, and due to the absence of car seats, Abel treated the van like his own personal jungle gym. We decided it would be best for Brian and the boys to have a relaxing day at the hotel while I made the journey alone. We said our goodbyes, and I reminded Brian that once I left the hotel I wouldn't be able to contact him from my cell phone unless I had Wi-Fi. I anxiously loaded into the van with a new guide I had never met and a driver, and then we began the long drive south.

After six very quiet hours in the car, we arrived in the city where Abel had been found and ultimately placed in the local orphanage. We were a little early for our scheduled appointment, so we pulled over to grab a quick bite to eat. As we were sitting at the small table eating, the guide looked up and casually said, "I heard your boy tested positive for TB."

Her accent was strong, and I was very tired, so I just stared at her for what was probably considered a rude amount of time.

"Wh-what?" I finally let out in an exasperated voice.

"Your guide called and told me that your boy tested positive, so she was going to the hotel to pick up your family and take them to the hospital to have more testing." She took a bite before continuing. "That was this morning, though, so they are already back at the hotel, and the scans came back clear, so you will still able to take him home with you."

Seriously? I should have known when our guide described the chances as "rare" and "less than 1 percent"—looked like Abel was going to fit into our family just fine. I tried to regain my composure and then frantically searched for Wi-Fi service—no luck. My conversation with Brian would have to wait.

We loaded back into the van and drove a few blocks down to see Abel's "finding place." I held my breath and tried to keep my composure as I stood in the spot where my very sick newborn son had been abandoned and ultimately found. As I looked around, my heart broke into a million pieces for his birthparents and for Abel. Adoption begins with such unimaginable tragedy, and in that moment, I was feeling the full weight of it. Most people want to just gloss over the pain that adoption stems from, but that would be doing our children a disservice. Abel had been left with a birth note; it hadn't contained any details at the risk of the birthparents being discovered, but written on a small piece of paper had been his birthdate and time of birth. His exact time of birth—that is a special detail that a loving mother remembers, a mother who deeply cares. We will never know the circumstances that led Abel to the orphanage, but I will never for one moment doubt that his first mother loved him and wanted a better life and good medical care for her child.

With a heavy heart, I climbed back into my seat and shut the van door. I was thankful that there was no expectation of conversation on this long journey. We drove another ten minutes until we arrived at the gates of the orphanage. This place had been my son's home for over two years.

As I explained in the chapter about Esme and her adoption story, I want to protect pieces of Abel's story as well. This part of the story is his to share when and if he is ever ready. I will say this, though, before I move on—that hour that I walked the halls of the social welfare institute was *hard*, but I left the building that day with my chin up at the thought that Abel would never be back there. He was no longer an orphan or a statistic—he was a son, a brother, a grandson, a nephew, a cousin—153 million orphans. Minus one.

The next few days were much less eventful—no more unexpected hospital trips. We made the effort to be tourists while we waited for our scheduled appointment at the consulate. We took the boys to the safari park to see the famous triplet pandas, we went hiking up a well-known viewpoint, but the air quality was so poor we couldn't see anything at the peak, and we walked around the outdoor spice market where we did a lot of looking but no buying—I had to remind Brian and Davis of this when we came upon a large bucket of live scorpions.

Finally, on January 17, we put on our best (yet travel-friendly) clothes, packed up our file of official documents, and headed to the US consulate for our scheduled appointment. This was the last step before we could go home. It was quick and painless, and even though we had to wait two more days for our official clearance, I went back to the hotel after the appointment and began packing up our things. I was ready to go home.

I painfully missed Rory and Esme. I missed my dog Rhett. I missed my bed. I missed clean air and tap water. And I missed meals that did not contain noodles. It was time to go home and be a family.

On January 19, we received Abel's passport to leave China. We were flying out of Hong Kong because we needed a direct flight to the United States. Abel could not land anywhere but American soil. The flight home was long and difficult with a child who was not only exhausted and overwhelmed but also not comforted by physical touch of any kind. He did not want to be held or soothed. He just wanted space, which is a bit of a dilemma on an international flight. In a desperate attempt to help Abel relax, I asked a flight attendant if Abel could lay on the floor. Honestly, I think she would have said yes to letting him hang from the ceiling as long as it meant that there were no screaming babies on the journey. With her permission, I gathered multiple airline blankets and pillows and created a comfy nest on the floor. We had four seats in a row and one seat that was now completely unoccupied by Abel so the nest actually offered Abel quite a bit of space to lie down and stretch out. He happily played, ate snacks, and even napped for about twenty minutes until finally the captain came over the loud speaker and announced that it was time to buckle up and prepare for landing. I whispered a prayer of gratitude.

* * *

After seven months of adoption paperwork, two weeks in China and twenty-seven hours of travel back to the States, we were finally home with Abel—and then the true work began.

Each morning, I get out of bed at 5:00 a.m. to be able to sit and type out this story—because if you have been paying attention at all, you will remember that we now have a bunch of kids so there are not a lot of quiet moments in our days. But as I sit here this morning sipping my coffee, I realized that today marks exactly five months since "Gotcha Day"—the day Abel joined our family. With that reflection I feel a flood of mixed emotions. On one hand, I think, how in the world has it only been five months? We have done so much, and Abel has grown and progressed more than I ever could have imagined. And on the other hand, I think it feels like so much more than only five short months because I can't seem to remember life without Abel or visualize our family before he was here. He is our son.

The last five months have been busy. Abel's medical file from China was a disaster, so we had to start over on everything. We have been working tirelessly with international adoption specialists, pediatric cardiologists, craniofacial specialists, ophthalmologists, audiologists, neurologists, speech therapists, physical therapists, endocrinologists, and our amazing family doctor to get Abel the medical care he needs. Through many hours of exams and medication and surgery, we are seeing our little man thrive. His cleft palate was surgically repaired in April, his blood disease has been labeled "compatible with life" and will not require blood transfusions as we had planned, his heart defect has—wait for it—"self-repaired," no liver damage has been found, he is now caught up on his vaccinations, he had tubes put in his ears so he can actually hear, and he has completed month four of nine months of his medication for latent TB. We are still working through a lot of medical issues and emotional trauma and have a long way to go, but the point is that we are doing it together as a family.

As an adoptive mother, it is difficult to miss your child's "firsts," but Abel has gifted us with some of those special moments as well. Only six weeks after Abel joined our family, he took his first steps. Brian and I sat on the living room floor, letting Abel take proud, wobbly sidesteps back and forth between us while Davis, Rory, and Esme all cheered him on. Abel joyfully clapped for himself *every* time he arrived into our arms. He also spoke his very first word (Mandarin or English) when he looked at me and said, "Mama," with a smile on his face—there's a very good chance he just wanted me to give him a snack, but still these are not moments I will take for granted. This is what it is all about. Adoption is not about a rescue; it is about being a family.

We have had a front-row seat to watching God work in big ways, and we would have missed all this if we'd let our comfort get in the way. Comfort is a tool of the enemy. Don't let that fool you. One of the passive-aggressive questions we received quite often before Abel came home was, "Won't this be difficult on your other children?" And the honest answer was yes, absolutely. This process has been taxing on the entire family in many ways, but that by no means indicates that it was not exactly what God was asking us to do. It meant that we needed and still need to keep our eyes fixed on Christ. We need to listen to His voice and not that of the world.

Now that the adoption is complete, when people learn about Abel's story, they immediately turn to us, raise their eyebrows, and say "Wow, you're amazing! Good for you!" But here's the thing—Brian and I are not amazing. We are not special or more qualified. We are not perfect people, and we are certainly *not* perfect parents. The bottom line is that we are just doing our best to follow Christ, and that means saying yes to the hard things that He calls us to.

God normally doesn't take into account how people feel about their callings. He just asks us to trust Him and then make it happen. Moses argued with God and told Him he was not capable of speaking well enough for the job he was chosen for. He didn't feel qualified to lead the Israelites out of Egypt—he even asked God to use someone else. Let's think for a moment about if Moses had walked away from the burning bush saying, "Seriously, God, no, thanks. It just sounds *too* hard." Queen Esther was full of self-doubt and fear at the task that God had handed her. She tried to justify a way out of her calling until she was reminded of the fact that possibly she was in the exact position she was in "for such a time as this" (Esther 4:14). Jonah made a run for it after God gave him a job, and we all know how God handled that one. God isn't looking for great people to work through, He is looking for surrendered people.

So maybe it's time to stop running from our callings and just *surrender*.

8 THE CALL TO ACTION

As I come to the end of my story (for now) I want to leave you with three important points—or calls to action. These are the reasons I felt compelled to write the pages of this book, and if you have made it this far in my story, then hopefully you will agree with me on the weight of their importance.

1—Confirm where you have built your foundation because the storms will in fact come.

I believe with my whole heart that Christ is infinitely important, and therefore, I have built my foundation on the rock rather than on the sand of this world. But here's the thing: I don't want my house to be all alone; I want an entire village on that rock! Do you have Christ?

If not, there is no better time to start because the storms of this life will come and Christ will be, and *wants* to be, your shelter.

Romans 10:9–11 (NIV) says, "If you declare with your mouth, 'Jesus is Lord,' and believe in your heart that God raised him from the dead, you will be saved. For it is with your heart that you believe and are justified, and it is with your mouth that you profess your faith and are saved." As Scripture says, "Anyone who believes in him will never be put to shame."

Along with accepting and knowing Christ comes an eternal perspective. Suddenly my pain, my battles, and even my life here on earth are brief in the big picture. Second Corinthians 4:16–18 (NIV) says, "Therefore we do not lose heart. Though outwardly we are wasting away, yet inwardly we are being renewed day by day. For our light and momentary troubles are achieving for us an eternal glory that far outweighs them all. So we fix our eyes not on what is seen, but on what is unseen, since what is seen is temporary, but what is unseen is eternal."

When we have Christ, the battles we are facing are just temporary, and a day is coming when He will mend every battle wound and scar. Revelation 21:4 (NLT) says, "He will wipe every tear from their eyes, and there will be no more death or sorrow or crying or pain. All these things are gone forever."

So let's fix our eyes on our leader because the reality is that even if it feels like we are losing the battle, Christ has already won the war.

Do not lose heart.

2—Have faith that God is still good even when life does not feel good.

If you ever, for even a moment, have doubt that God is using our suffering for good and for growth then consider the story of Joseph. Let me just stop here and take a moment to summarize Joseph's life from Genesis chapters 37–50.

> Joseph and his father Jacob lived in Canaan. Joseph was seventeen at the time this story starts, and he had ten older brothers. Joseph was his father's favorite son, and therefore, Jacob gifted him a special robe. In true sibling fashion, this did not make Joseph's brothers very happy.
>
> One day, Joseph had a dream, and unfortunately for him, he told his brothers about it. He explained to them that in the dream Joseph and his brothers were tying up bunches of grain out in the field when suddenly Joseph's grain raised up while all of his brother's grain gathered around and bowed down to it. The brothers didn't seem to appreciate this dream, but Joseph continued. He then described a second dream where the sun, moon, and eleven stars bowed down to Joseph.
>
> To say that the brothers were not pleased with Joseph's dreams would be a drastic understatement.
>
> A few days later, Joseph's father asked him to check on his brothers while they were working in the fields quite far off. When the brothers saw Joseph in

the distance, they made a plan to kill him. Joseph's oldest brother heard this and suggested that they just throw him into the empty well instead—nice guy.

So when Joseph arrived, they stole his robe, and they threw him into the well. Shortly after, a caravan headed to Egypt came by, and the brothers decided that instead of killing Joseph, they would just sell him into slavery instead. Then the kind brothers took Joseph's robe and dipped it in animal blood and told their father that Joseph had been killed by an animal.

So poor Joseph was taken to Egypt where he started out as a slave but then was falsely imprisoned for several years. Seriously, things are not going well for Joseph.

The prison warden decided to put Joseph in charge of all the prisoners. After Joseph had been in jail for some time the pharaoh's cupbearer and baker were also imprisoned with Joseph. One night, each of them had a dream. They told their dreams to Joseph, and he interpreted each dream for them. Joseph explained that the dreams showed that the cupbearer would soon be let out of jail and Joseph then asked for the cupbearer to tell Pharaoh about him.

When the cupbearer was released he forgot all about Joseph. So Joseph remained in jail. Two years later, the pharaoh had a dream, and nobody could explain it to him. The cupbearer then remembered what Joseph had done for him, and Joseph was summoned to Pharaoh.

After Pharaoh told Joseph his dream, Joseph explained that it was a warning from God that there would be seven years of abundance followed by seven years of extreme famine. Pharaoh believed everything that Joseph told him, and put him in charge of all of Egypt—finally things were looking up for Joseph.

Joseph saved a portion of the harvest over the seven years of abundance to prepare for the famine so that when it came, they would still have food for the people of Egypt. When the famine came, people traveled from all over to buy grain from Joseph. Some of those hungry people in need were Joseph's very own brothers. When his brothers arrived, they all bowed to Joseph because he was now an important person, just as he had dreamed they would at the beginning. Joseph recognized them, but they did not recognize him because it had been many years.

After some time Joseph told his brothers and his father who he was, and he even offered his forgiveness. So his father, his brothers, and their families came to live in Egypt with Joseph, and they had all the food they needed.

Joseph was almost murdered by his own brothers, he was thrown into an empty well, he was sold into slavery in Egypt, and then as if that all wasn't bad enough, he was falsely imprisoned for years. I've never personally experienced any of these things, so I can only imagine how discouraged Joseph must have felt. I would also imagine that he would have an excuse to become bitter because of his circumstances. But do you know what he said to his brothers when he finally revealed himself to them at the end of the story in Genesis 50:20 (NIV)?

> You intended to harm me, but God intended it for good to accomplish what is now being done, the saving of many lives.

Joseph had faith that God was in control, and even when God did not take his suffering away, Joseph knew that God was still good. He understood that God was using his suffering, and through that very suffering, God used Joseph to save an entire people group.

Never doubt that God is at work. We might not understand His plans, but we can still have faith that God is good, and He is strengthening us through our battles. So let go of the anger, the bitterness, the anxiety, or whatever else you are carrying around through life. Give it to God. Chin up and soldier on. God's got this—God's got you.

3—Shout your battle cry!

This, my friends, is the whole point of the book.

> battle cry: (noun) a loud shout given by soldiers to
> frighten the enemy or to encourage their own side

It is time to shout our own personal battle cries and to do that we must start sharing our stories—the real and the messy and the broken ones. It is time to encourage one another. And for goodness' sake, it is definitely time to push back the enemy!

Even if people don't want to talk about it the fact of the matter is that the enemy is real—*very real*. First Peter 5:8–9 (NIV) says, "Your enemy the Devil prowls around like a roaring lion looking for someone to devour." I don't know about you, but I kind of want to be ready for something like that! The verse continues, saying, "Resist him, standing firm in the faith, because you know that the family of believers throughout the world is undergoing the same kind of suffering." We are not alone in this fight—so let's stop acting like it!

Isaiah 43:2 (NIV) says,

> When you pass through the waters,
> I will be with you;
> and when you pass through the rivers, they will not sweep over you.
> When you walk through the fire, you will not be burned;
> the flames will not set you ablaze.

Notice that the verse does not promise that God will dry up the waters or reroute the river or even put out the fire. No, He says, "I will be with you," *in* the roaring waters and raging rivers and blazing fires.

He protects us and fights for us. He consistently shows up. He does the work in our lives—with us and through us. And then what do we do? We just quietly move on with life as if we somehow saved ourselves. Well, it is time to stop. When we are too afraid to share our stories, God misses the glory that He is due. Our lives are God's *battle cry*—our story is *His* victory! We were never created to be the heroes of our own stories. We were created to be the *rescued*.

So let's stop living small. Let's fight big!

Let's raise our voices and share our stories.

Let's encourage one another and push back the enemy.

It's time to shout our battle cry and give God the glory He is due.

Who's with me?

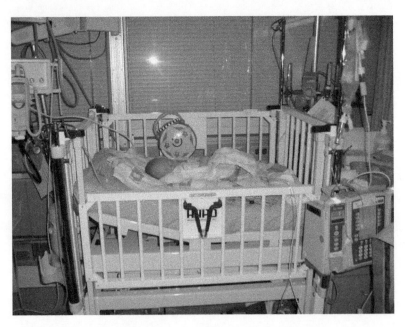

Davis in the Neonatal Intensive Care Unit

Davis being loaded into the airplane to go back to OHSU

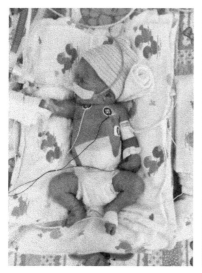
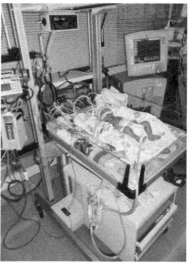

Rory in the Neonatal Intensive Care Unit

Candid moment with Rory and Davis (ages two & three- and-a-half years)

Davis and Rory meeting Esme in the hospital for the first time

Rory holding the baby kangaroo at breakfast in the hotel

Watching Jack Hanna's cheetah walk through the hotel lobby

The journey home from Ohio

Finalizing Esme's adoption at the courthouse
in Ohio when she was six months old

Our family of five

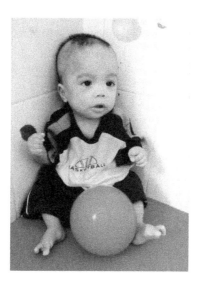

Profile picture as "Noah"
This is the first picture we ever saw of Abel.

The day we finalized Abel's adoption at the civil-affairs office in Guangzhou, China

The room Abel slept in at the orphanage in China

Exploring the market in China

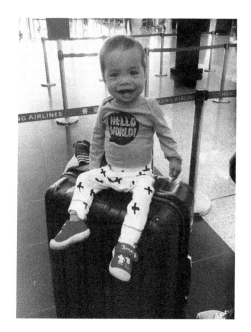

Leaving China and heading to the United States

Abel's Early Intervention school photo at nine months home

Our family of six

Davis, age eight

Rory, age seven

Esme, age three

Abel and Esme

Esme and Brian

Davis, Esme, Rory, and Abel

Battle Verses

Consider it pure joy, my brothers and sisters, whenever you face trials of many kinds, because you know that the testing of your faith produces perseverance. Let perseverance finish its work so that you may be mature and complete, not lacking anything.

—James 1:2–4 (NIV)

Not only so, but we also glory in our sufferings, because we know that suffering produces perseverance; perseverance character; and character, hope. And hope does not put us to shame, because God's love has been poured out into our hearts through the Holy Spirit, who has been given to us.

—Roman 5:3–5 (NIV)

Finally, be strong in the Lord and in his mighty power. Put on the full armor of God, so that you can take your stand against the devil's schemes. For our struggle is not against flesh and blood, but against the rulers, against the authorities, against the powers of this dark world and against the spiritual forces of evil in the heavenly realms. Therefore put on the full armor of God, so that when the day of evil comes, you may be able to stand your ground, and after you have done everything, to stand. Stand firm then, with the belt of truth buckled around your waist, with the breastplate of righteousness in place, and with your feet fitted with the readiness that comes from the gospel of peace. In addition to all this, take up the shield of faith, with which you can extinguish all the flaming arrows of the evil one. Take up the helmet of salvation and the sword of the Spirit, which is the word of God.

—Ephesians 6:10–17 (NIV)

Therefore we do not lose heart. Though outwardly we are wasting away, yet inwardly we are being renewed day by day. For our light and momentary troubles are achieving for us an eternal glory that far outweighs them all. So we fix our eyes not on what is seen, but what is unseen, since what is seen is temporary, but what is unseen is eternal.

—2 Corinthians 4:16–18 (NIV)

The Lord is my shepherd, I lack nothing.
He makes me lie down in green pastures,
he leads me beside quiet waters,
he refreshes my soul.
He guides me along the right paths for his name's sake.

Even though I walk through the darkest valley,

I will fear no evil,

for you are with me;

your rod and staff,

they comfort me.

You prepare a table before me in the presence of my

enemies.

You anoint my head with oil;

my cup overflows.

Surely your goodness and love will follow me all the

days of my life,

and I will dwell in the house of the Lord forever.

—Psalm 23 (NIV)

Do you not know? Have you not heard? The Lord is the everlasting God, the Creator of the ends of the earth. He will not grow tired or weary, and his understanding no one can fathom. He gives strength to the weary and increases the power of the weak. Even youths grow tired and weary, and young men stumble and fall; but those who hope in the Lord will renew their strength. They will soar on wings like eagles; they will run and not grow weary, they will walk and not be faint.

—Isaiah 40:28–31 (NIV)

But he said to me, "My grace is sufficient for you, for my power is made perfect in weakness." Therefore I will boast all the more gladly about my weaknesses, so that Christ's power may rest on me. That is why, for Christ's sake, I delight in weaknesses, in insults, in hardships, in persecutions, in difficulties. For when I am weak, then I am strong.

—2 Corinthians 12:9–10 (NIV)

God is our refuge and strength, an ever-present help in trouble. Therefore we will not fear, though the earth give way and the mountains fall into the heart of the sea, though its waters roar and foam and the mountains quake with their surging.

—Psalm 46:1–3 (NIV)

God is within her, she will not fall; God will help her at break of day.

—Psalm 46:5 (NIV)

The Lord is my strength and my shield; my heart trusts in him, and he helps me. My heart leaps for joy, and with my song I praise him. The Lord is the strength of his people, a fortress of salvation for his anointed one.

—Psalm 28:7–8 (NIV)

Who shall separate us from the love of Christ? Shall trouble or hardship or persecution or famine or nakedness or danger or sword? As it is written: "For your sake we face death all day long; we are considered as sheep to be slaughtered." No, in all these things we are more than conquerors through him who loved us. For I am convinced that neither death nor life, neither angels nor demons, neither the present nor the future, nor any powers, neither height nor depth, nor anything else in all creation, will be able to separate us from the love of God that is in Christ Jesus our Lord.

—Romans 8:35–39 (NIV)

The Lord is my light and my salvation—whom shall I fear? The Lord is the stronghold of my life—of whom shall I be afraid?

—Psalm 27:1 (NIV)

For I am the Lord your God who takes hold of your right hand and says to you, Do not fear; I will help you.

—Isaiah 41:13 (NIV)

Join with me in suffering, like a good soldier of Christ Jesus. No one serving as a soldier gets entangled in civilian affairs, but rather tries to please his commanding officer.

—2 Timothy 2:3–4 (NIV)

Cast all your anxiety on him because he cares for you.

—1 Peter 5:7 (NIV)

I can do all this through him who gives me strength.

—Phil 4:13 (NIV)

Blessed is the one who perseveres under trial because, having stood the test, that person will receive the

crown of life that the Lord has promised to those
who love him.

—James 1:12 (NIV)

But now, this is what the Lord says—
he who created you, Jacob,
he who formed you, Israel:
"Do no fear, for I have redeemed you;
I have summoned you by name; you are mine.
When you pass through the waters,
I will be with you;
and when you pass through the rivers,
they will not sweep over you.
When you walk through the fire,
you will not be burned;
the flames will not set you ablaze."

—Isaiah 43:1-2 (NIV)

And we know that in all things God works for the
good of those who love him, who have been called
according to his purpose.

—Romans 8:28 (NIV)

Trust in the Lord with all your heart and lean not on
your own understanding; in all your ways submit to
him and he will make your paths straight.

—Proverbs 3:5–6 (NIV)

What, then, shall we say in response to these things?
If God is for us, who can be against us?

—Romans 8:31 (NIV)

Lord, be gracious to us;
we long for you.
Be our strength every morning,
our salvation in time of distress.

—Isaiah 33:2 (NIV)

The Lord himself goes before you and will be with
you; he will never leave you nor forsake you. Do not
be afraid; do not be discouraged.

—Deuteronomy 31:8 (NIV)

He will wipe every tear from their eyes, and there
will be no more death or sorrow or crying or pain.
All these things are gone forever.

—Revelation 21:4 (NLT)

CPSIA information can be obtained
at www.ICGtesting.com
Printed in the USA
LVHW112104270519
619129LV00001B/11/P